ENJOYING THE PARENTING ROLLER COASTER

Nurturing and Empowering Your Children through the Ups and Downs

Marie Masterson, PhD, and Katharine Kersey, EdD

Gryphon House
www.gryphonhouse.com

Bulk Purchase
Gryphon House books are available for special premiums and sales promotions as well as for fund-raising use. Special editions or book excerpts also can be created to specifications. For details, call 800.638.0928.

Disclaimer
Gryphon House, Inc. cannot be held responsible for damage, mishap, or injury incurred during the use of or because of activities in this book. Appropriate and reasonable caution and adult supervision of children involved in activities and corresponding to the age and capability of each child involved are recommended at all times. Do not leave children unattended at any time. Observe safety and caution at all times.

ENJOYING THE PARENTING ROLLER COASTER

Nurturing and Empowering Your Children through the Ups and Downs

Marie Masterson, PhD, and Katharine Kersey, EdD

TABLE OF CONTENTS

ACKNOWLEDGEMENTS

Thank you to the amazing moms who shared their personal stories, insights, and laughter, especially Sarah Duncan, Kate Harris Oberjuerge, Mallory Rheins Crist, Lisa Masterson, and Sara Masterson Smith. Thank you to Katharine for encouraging me to write this parenting book and allowing me to use the strategies that were the focus of my research and our previous book. Thank you to my spiritual guides and dearest friends who have heaped my own parenting journey with prayer and cheering, especially Sandy Gonnering, Jana Howard, and Jerianne Thielecke. Most of all, thank you to the ones I love most, my children, David, James, Sara, and Steve, and their beautiful families. You are my heroes in this life, my heart, my inspiration, and the ones I aspire most to be like. Every day with you has been my greatest joy.

INTRODUCTION

Whether you are a new parent who desires a deeper understanding of your child, an experienced parent who wants to build more meaningful relationships with your family, or a struggling parent on the verge of desperation, this book will inspire you and give you the practical help to make parenting the joy it is meant to be. Instead of getting bogged down in cycles of frustration, you will leave behavior struggles behind and turn children on to cooperation and respect. You will be able to maximize the influence of your relationship and become your own best self—as you show your children how to live.

In each chapter, you will find quick and helpful strategies that show what works, with parent perspectives that reveal daily struggles and successes, challenges and insights. Each section is power-packed with tools and resources to help you recharge your energy; boost your skills; and give you words, actions, and activities to put into use right away. The practical tips are filled with advice that will positively affect your daily life and relationships with your child and others who matter to you. You can explore one section at a time or investigate the chapters by topic in any order that meets the need of your own unique parenting journey. As you read, you will find a philosophy of respectful, relational parenting that will change your child's life and your own.

CHAPTER 1
ANCHORING YOUR PARENTING HEART

Beginning the Adventure

Becoming a parent is like walking into the most powerful love ever felt. But in the beginning, it can feel overwhelming. On top of the pressure you may feel from others, it's common to put even more pressure on yourself. You may have waited a long time. You want to do everything right. In the first few weeks, the best idea is to put aside your plan, try to relax, and get a little sleep. Enjoy lots of snuggles. The rest will fall into place.*

You may have had thirty hours of labor. Maybe your child came to you through months of planning to secure paperwork for adoption from another country. Maybe you are the busy parent of multiples who needs uncommon energy. Perhaps you adopted siblings or older children who need patience and love. Maybe this child came when least expected and altered your plans. As all of us discover as we embark on the journey, parenthood changes your life.

*Editor's Note: Highlighted throughout the book are unattributed quotes that offer personal perspectives on parenting. They are not intended to be from any particular individual but are, instead, compilations of responses that the author has received from many different parents. They reflect perspectives commonly held by many individuals.

Perhaps everyone has given you advice: Feed on demand. Put him on a schedule. Comfort him immediately. Don't pick him up right away. Put him down while he is awake. Place him in bed asleep. Use a swing. Don't rely on a swing, or he won't fall asleep any other way. Not only is this child missing an instruction manual, but the information offered by others often conflicts.

If you're lucky, you have close friends with children. You can watch what they do and take notes on what you like or declare with certainty what you will never do. You may wonder if you have what it takes to do parenting well. You may wish your childbirth classes would give more information about how to be a parent—after the baby arrives. You may wonder what you'll do when your sweet baby turns into a tantrum-prone toddler, an inconsolable preschooler, or an eight-year-old with attitude.

As children grow, parents often waste a great deal of energy trying to stop misbehavior. You stop it today, but it starts up again tomorrow. Parents often fall into a cycle of negative focus and frustration and never really figure out a different approach. We see this all around us in restaurants and malls: parents at their wits' end, and children who are discouraged. Many people think that the most important factor in getting children to behave is the child. The truth is that your own actions and words have tremendous influence on behavior. In fact, what you say and do can radically influence your child's response. You need effective skills to get your child to do something when needed—and to turn a situation around when necessary.

With positive relational guidance, you can learn how to come alongside your child to inspire and enable success. Instead of stepping into power struggles, you can understand how to boost cooperation and build needed strengths. Your child will tune in to you and become sensitive to your influence. You'll spend less energy yet get the results you want.

Something else happens that is priceless. Positive guidance entirely reorients your role in your child's life. You become the kind of parent you really want to be—joyful and confident—with a child who is fun to be around and happy with himself. Your child will become self-directed, requiring less time from you to attend to behavior issues. Instead, you spend more time accomplishing your real goal—empowering your child to take control of his life in meaningful and healthy ways.

It is easy to feel overwhelmed with sleep-interrupted nights and responsibilities to juggle. It helps to keep a clear perspective. Understanding your remarkable influence in the life of your child opens the door to make parenting all you hope for—a satisfying and fulfilling adventure. When these years have passed and you look back on the memories, only one thing will matter most: having created a close and loving relationship with your child—one that will keep you connected for life.

Mastering the Care and Feeding—of You

After the birth of my first child, I struggled with my emotions, and my physical pain was exacerbated by that struggle. I realized it wasn't just me who was trying to learn to nurse; it was my baby, too. Some friends reminded me to give myself lots of grace during this period and to take time to adjust. It helped to think of parenting as something my baby and I needed to figure out together.

For some people, parenting feels natural and satisfying. For others, it takes time to figure out patterns and routines that feel right. You need a comfortable amount of space, privacy, and help—in ways that work well for you. The more secure you feel about your choices, the sooner you can relax and settle in. The key to a successful approach is to realize that what you do may not be the same as what others do. Make decisions about the practical issues that will work best for yourself and for your family.

It will take time to get into a regular rhythm. There are some things that lie outside of your influence, but there is also a lot that you can control. It helps to make a mental list of what matters to you and what does not. Things will go much more easily if you let go of the nonessentials and keep your expectations realistic.

When you feel frazzled, want to calm the chaos, or simply need a workable plan of action, it helps to have some practical steps in mind, especially for the first six weeks after the child comes home. Get back to basics and make sure that things work in a way that helps you thrive and not simply get by. The following strategies are essential for new parents and remain critical as children get older:

- **Take emergency and planned refreshers.** A five-minute break can energize and renew the body, mind, and spirit. Listen to music that makes you feel happy. Keep an inspirational book in the bathroom. Take short naps at every opportunity. Eat and rehydrate on schedule to nourish and renew so that you can be the best you.

- **Communicate well.** Effective teamwork takes practice. Talk ahead of time with your spouse or partner about what would help you the most. Be clear about what you want. Give specific instructions if you care how something is done. Be direct, so that others can feel effective in the ways they support you. Your gratitude will be genuine.

- **If you need help, get it.** Whether you need assistance with an errand or food delivered, don't wait until you feel desperate or out of sorts. If something doesn't work one day, make quick adjustments to get what you need rather than repeating yesterday's plan in the hope that things will turn out differently. A proactive mindset will make all the difference.

- **Speak up.** Don't be hesitant when talking with your lactation consultant, doctor, or pediatrician. Describe what you observe and what you want to know in detail. If you don't understand something, keep asking questions until you feel satisfied. Having adequate knowledge and resources will help you design an effective plan for the health and well-being of your child.

- **Protect your need for space.** If you need privacy, be sure to ask for it. If you don't want visitors right away when the child is born or comes home, say, "Thanks so much for caring. I look forward to spending time with you soon." Not everyone is comfortable figuring out things with others around. Set boundaries to protect your energy.

- **Maximize resources.** Reach out to parent-support groups, child and family services, and community and faith organizations. Find websites that suit your style and sense of humor. Make use of all available options to find information, inspiration, and encouragement.

- **Take notes.** Keep data on feeding and sleep schedules. Record what works and what doesn't. Write down questions and to-do notes as things cross your mind. Keep track of details when your child is ill. You can use these records when you visit the pediatrician or talk to others for advice.

- **Build relationships.** Parenting is not an isolation sport. Make friends in your parenting class if you are new to your area. Renew relationships with others who are parents you admire. Reach out to families at the local library, YMCA, or house of worship. Having people around you is so important. You need a support system to bounce around ideas, share goals, and talk with when what you are doing is not working—and when things are going well. Nurturing friendships and keeping them strong will lead to more fun and helpful solutions to problems.

- **Laugh a lot.** Nothing helps more than to realize that you can't do much about spit up on your shirt except change the shirt and move on. Just laugh and remind yourself that this, too, will pass. Laughing releases positive endorphins and will make you feel better when challenging moments come.

Keeping a clear perspective helps you stay aware and sensitive to your child and to yourself. Start with the care and feeding—of you. Honor your needs. Nurturing yourself and your partner will set a lasting pattern for ongoing health and happiness.

Gaining Insight into Your Emotions

When I was growing up, our family had pleasant dinner conversations. If anyone started talking about something negative, my dad would clear his throat and we would know to change the subject. I love that I had that protected space.

Many people know families that they want to emulate. Others may worry that they cannot be all that they hope to for their children. You may have role models in your past that you don't want to be like or who weren't able to give the love and nurturing you really needed. No matter what background you had, you can be a good parent. The lessons you have learned from your own life can now give you vision and determination to create a strong and healthy home.

Each family is unique. Maybe you were raised in a home where everyone covered up, but you married someone who runs around in a towel—or less. It may be that you talk openly about your feelings, but your significant other broods and doesn't get to the point. You may have a short fuse, and your partner may be the most patient person you know. Maybe you have a close, safe relationship with your own family, or perhaps you really need more distance. Reflecting on the past can give tremendous insight as you decide what will work best for you today.

Some people have experienced abuse as children. A dad reflected, "I think my parents spanked because they didn't know what else to do. They had a misguided belief that it helped. Instead, I felt hurt and angry. I want to raise my children with respect and love and use high expectations but not pain. Our children are now four and eight and have never been spanked. They are the sweetest, most thoughtful girls. I love that I changed the pattern. We did it together."

A mom said, "I was teased by my brothers and was determined to protect my own children. My mom was critical of my hair and clothes, so I let my daughter express herself. My father gave us the silent treatment, and even though I said I would never be like that, I find myself closing up when I feel upset. I want to work on this pattern and change it."

Another mother shared this perspective. "When I grew up, I didn't have a mom. My childhood held a great deal of anxiety. But when I became a mother, I realized that my friends were trying to be like their moms. I understood that I had the freedom to make this relationship with my children work in a way that was good for me. I never resented putting my children to bed or the sleep-deprived nights, because I knew what it was like not to have that kind of care. My past has made me grateful for every moment I have today. I appreciate the boys and love being able to nurture them. Because I didn't have the love I wanted, I treasure being able to give it to my children."

When you become a parent, you have the opportunity to choose. You can create life as you want it to be and become the kind of person you aspire to be. Talk with your partner and other significant people helping to raise your child, and together figure out a path that works for you. What really matters is the stability, faith, hope, and love that you bring forward.

> Treat the child the same way you do other important people in your life—the way you want him to treat you and others. Think before you speak: How would you want him to say that to you?

Keep a journal and record experiences that go well for you. Take notes about areas that raise unfinished business. Some parents write poetry or prayers that reflect their hopes and commitments. Talk to a good friend or visit a professional counselor or clergy member if you find you want to understand and solve problems that revisit you often or if you desire healing for past experiences. Your children will benefit from your determination to be a truly healthy role model.

Understanding the Power of Your Influence

Memories of The Nutcracker *and other holiday traditions meant a lot to me growing up. But the first time we planned a sleigh ride for our girls, I was so stressed getting out the door that I was still tense as we bundled together on the sleigh and the horses started down the road. I could feel my daughter looking up at me. She was watching to see if I was having fun. There may be times when your plans sound good, but the reality doesn't match your ideal.*

The root of empathy for yourself may have been affected by the way someone once spoke to you. "I am relaxed and can take things as they come, but when I am late, I feel so anxious!" a busy mom shared. "I remember how my dad would get upset with us when we were late. I am really trying to reorient that message with my own children." Making connections to the past can give us positive determination to speak kindly and be gentle with ourselves and our children in the present.

Respect can only truly be given to others when it is rooted in respect for the self. This begins in the way you talk to (and about) yourself. In the grocery-store aisle, you might mumble, "I'm an idiot. I left my shopping list at home." In the coffee shop, you might say, "I want a cookie, but I'm going to have to run three miles to make up for it." If you speak this way to yourself when your child is present, he sees and hears these messages.

What would happen if your child heard you say instead, "I left the grocery list at home. Can you help me remember what we need?" Or in the coffee shop: "I have been look-ing forward to my time with you. Why don't you pick out a cookie for yourself, and choose one for me? I will love whatever you decide." Wow. The world would be buzz-ing with positive feelings of respect if we all talked like that.

Children internalize the words they hear. Your affirmations or criticisms become their inner voice. They remember the experiences that make them feel competent or inept. They internalize a mindset of compassion or complaint based on the patterns set, often inadvertently, for them. Think carefully about and become purposeful in how you respond. It is important to see how your own actions and words can influence your child's developing life perspective.

One father said, "Treat your kids with respect. It seems simple enough, but it's not. As a parent, you feel that you are the boss. What you say goes. And while that can be true, your child is still a little person with a little soul who hears and absorbs anything and everything that you do."

Treat children the way you want to be treated—with respect and kindness. To do this, you need to set your inner voice to renewed empathy and acceptance. Write out a positive affirmation and post it in a visible place to remind yourself to stay grounded in respect. Accepting and valuing children begins with the determination to accept and value ourselves.

Parenthood can motivate us to become more honest and thoughtful about the way we live, knowing that we are leaving a lasting legacy and impacting the direction of our children's lives. Like a hand pressed into wet cement, our words leave a positive or negative impression that hardens over time and changes the perception children have about themselves and the world. Keeping the camera on the amazing strength of your own influence in the lives of your children is at the heart of positive parenting.

Handling the Hard Work

My kids are driving me crazy. They've been home three days in a row. I want to yell at them when they are climbing all over the house. They are bored, and I am at my wit's end. Being a parent is really hard.

Parenting is one of the hardest jobs you'll ever do. In a typical day, you need a plastic mat under the highchair to catch spilled food, the laundry piles up, the babysitter calls in sick, and you need a break. Your three- and five-year-olds can't seem to stop squabbling, and the baby is teething. This day is going to require nerves of steel and determination.

Even more, you get little relief from constant requests. Someone needs you around the clock to soothe a hurt, give a kiss, wipe a bottom, and find a clean shirt or dry pajamas. When you're alone in the night rocking a teething baby, or when you're awakened at six in the morning by your preschooler, you may realize this is going to take a level of selflessness that you didn't know you had.

It is easy to get bogged down in the daily challenges, and some days will press your limits. Children have a way of letting us know what we are honestly made of. They reveal our true grit and make us dig deep for strength and faith. Your children's needs often will conflict with your own. It requires a lot of flexibility to make the best decision in the moment and to keep your priorities straight.

When you don't have time for a shower, can't get in the bathroom alone, and have already read their favorite books so many times that you can say the words by heart, you need a fresh perspective. This may be the time to scrap your plans, refocus attention, and tell yourself that you can do this. Be like the Little Engine That Could and repeat, "I think I can. I think I can," until you get through the day. Tomorrow, things really will feel better.

> Stay aware of your limits. Get support and help when you need it. Don't wait until things are out of control and you feel like you are in over your head.

Big journeys are made up of small steps. Some days will make you feel like being a parent is so easy. Other times, you'll feel certain that you're not up for the challenge. The following ideas can help you find renewed strength and stamina and will remind you to focus on maximizing each moment.

- **Be realistic.** Don't overshoot the schedule. Make plans, but be willing to let things go.

- **Find (or beg for) company.** Have a family member or a friend come over for an hour to give you a mental-health break and an extra hand.

- **Plan a play date.** Invite another mom. Let the children romp in the living room or take turns holding babies.

- **Switch it up.** Scrap the routine, pack up the lunch, and eat outside. If it is raining, have a picnic on a blanket indoors.

- **Be creative.** Let the children pretend to go on vacation in their bathing suits with the tub as their pool. Provide water crayons that rinse off the tub and tile. Have a pajama party and play in bed during the day.

- **Get out.** Take the children to the library, the children's museum, or to the park. Pack them into the stroller or wagon for a walk around the block. It is worth the effort of putting on jackets, coats, mittens, and boots to get a breath of fresh air. The change of pace will do you all good.

- **Escape with a purpose.** Visit a pet store or petting zoo to explore the animals. Infants and toddlers, especially, will learn so much. Older children can return home to draw and talk about the animals they saw.

- **Retreat.** Grab the blankets and pillows, and cuddle on the couch and read books together. Make a fort. Add pillows and flashlights, and snuggle underneath.

- **Find a helper.** Invite an older child over to play with your younger children for a few hours. The helper can set up craft time and snacks or hold the baby while you have time to focus on needed tasks.

- **Sleep when you can.** When you are a new parent, go to bed when the children go to bed, and nap when they nap. It is tempting to tackle needed work, but you will accomplish twice as much in half the time after a few minutes (or hours) of blissful rest.

When you're having a hard day, it helps to focus on the child in front of you and to think about the outcomes you want to achieve. Reaching out to others for help really makes a difference. It is reassuring to know that you are not alone in the parenting journey.

Surviving the Roller-Coaster Ride

Parenthood is the biggest emotional roller coaster you will ever ride. Some days you will feel like you have been on it forever. Some days the ride is over almost before you get your seatbelt fastened. Embrace the moment. Realize you will never be the same. From now on, you will always be thinking about what you can do to improve your child's life— today and for the future. Enjoy it all. Cry when you need to. Laugh a lot. Have faith. Remember that what your child really needs is your love.

A three-year old boy said, "I can tell when my mom is mad, because she walks like this!" He marched across the room with his feet wide and his hands on his hips. His facial expression looked just like hers. If you ask your children to "be you" and to show you what you look or sound like, you likely will be surprised at what they can do! They can capture Mom or Dad perfectly.

Even the best of us wish we could take back a moment gone wrong or rewind our words when frustrations happen. Children can tell right away if you are upset about something that just happened. You will have many moments that try your patience. When the toilet paper gets unrolled, the new crayons are used on the living-room wall, or that pretty flower arrangement has been pulled apart, recognize your limits and plan for better ways to handle things.

When you feel upset or frustrated, you can say, "I am sorry I got mad. Please forgive me. I wish I had been patient." When your child is upset, you can say, "I am sorry you're upset. I know you were playing. Let's read for a while together." It takes practice to manage the demands when you feel under pressure. Children forgive quickly, and they understand when things are frustrating.

Make sure you aren't living close to the emotional edge and that you keep a reservoir of strength and energy. When you are detached, children become clingier. When you are anxious, children become concerned. When you are rested, your reactions to everyone are gentler, your responses easier, and your temper less likely to be short. You will be able to handle the ups and downs when you've taken good care of yourself.

> Children pick up on our emotions and responses. They model our ways of handling feelings, so you want to do your best to be good examples of healthy behavior.

Taming Stress

The last three texts to my mom were, "Sorry can't talk now. Taking family pics and Aiden stepped in poop," "CU later, John is hollering at kids," and "Help! Dog ate dinner off table." My stress level is through the roof, and more often than not, something gives. I hate it when it's my patience.

With worry about finances, panic when you need to be in two places at once, interpersonal irritations, and lack of sleep, the pressures of raising children can pile up. Stress and children go hand in hand, and things are bound to be unpredictable. Staying connected as a family can help keep the bonds strong and flexible, so that you all work better together when things get rough. But ultimately, when stress becomes a pattern, it is time to decide what is important and what can be let go. Weed out the necessary from the optional.

- **Take a stress test.** Give yourself the "How painful is this?" test, like the one used in hospitals to gauge perceived pain. Keep track of your schedule, and assign a 1–10 rating for your stress level at various activities, with 10 representing unbearable stress and 1 signifying minimal stress. After several weeks, make a plan to change the way you handle the tasks and obligations that you rated consistently high in stress. If possible, let go of the high-stress activities.

- **Make small steps.** Don't make stress relief an all-or-nothing proposition. You can't ditch it all and take a vacation, and you can't keep up the pace. Instead, take five-minute exercise breaks to rejuvenate. Enforce a ten-minute quiet time, during which everyone hangs out together but doesn't talk. (Providing books and a snack may help.) Relax with your children, lying on the floor and listening to music to calm your nerves.

- **Maximize "now."** If you've been at work and have come home to chaos, let everything wait. Push aside the cleaning and the ringing phone and the piled-up mail, and spend some focused time together. Children will never remember the mess, but they will remember your hugs and attention. Put their feelings and spirits first.

- **Review weekly.** Hold a once-a-week review meeting—with yourself. If your family's stuff is piling up, put laundry baskets or cartons in those areas of the house. A contained mess feels less overwhelming than one that spreads out. You can tackle it later by the boxful.

- **Honor your way.** Stick to the kind of cleaning routine that works for you. If you prefer a weekly organizing binge, go for it. Or if it works better for you, complete one small project per day so that you stay on top of things. If you are not a daily mail opener, make sure it all heads to a single basket to be handled on Saturday morning over coffee.

- **Give yourself permission.** Accomplish just one of your top three chores. Let the other two go for today. Focus on the essentials.

- **Play office.** If you have "work" work to do, let children play office. Put a container or basket filled with markers, rulers, pencils, maze books, drawing books, tape, scissors, graph paper, and a clip board in your office space. They can sit with you and do their "work" while you do yours. Ask them to make a card or a sign for you.

They understand when you need to get things done. A little planning ahead can make all the difference.

- **Sit together.** When children are doing homework, sit with them to read, balance your checkbook, sort mail, or pay bills. It is a nice feeling to have your presence while they work, and you can share the quiet, focused time.

- **Add technology wisely.** For school-age children, educational games on a digital tablet can give you a few minutes to yourself. Just make this choice a now-and-then, special activity instead of your instant go-to. If you need critical work time on the computer, that's a good time to have children nearby "working" on their computer, too.

- **Keep emotional tanks filled.** Take a few minutes to tune in to your child's world. Before you shift your attention away to a necessary task, give a hug, spend a few minutes reading a book, or share a happy activity.

- **Try to keep things in perspective.** If you are safe, have a roof over your head, and your children are near, count those blessings. Breathe deeply, light a candle, pray, and repeat positive affirmations. Your child is learning from you how to handle tense moments and stressful interruptions. It will pay off for you to be able to keep calm and refocus your energy.

> Remember the importance of taking good care of yourself physically as well as emotionally. Eat well, sleep well, and get plenty of exercise. You will cope better and serve as a good role model for your children.

A dad at the end of his sanity said, "I heard this great quote about how being negative only makes a difficult journey more difficult. The author and speaker Joyce Meyer said, 'You may be given a cactus, but you don't have to sit on it!'" Accepting what is and then making the most of it is a skill that will change your child's life and your own. This perspective gives you the option to determine what happens to you rather than to taking on the role of victim. Show your children that the way you respond matters by not blaming on someone else all of the things that go wrong.

Taking Steps to Jump-Start Your Day

We were constantly late leaving in the morning, and my daughter kept melting down. I realized how much my own feelings were wearing off on her. When I calmed down, she calmed down. We decided to put a "go to school" box by the door, and make sure things were there the night before. Also, I started getting up ten minutes earlier. It was painful at first, but that little change made a big difference. I could give more attention to help her.

A positive morning routine can brighten the mood for the rest of the day. Nothing helps you feel so instantly great about being a parent like a morning routine that works or so discouraged about parenting when your morning doesn't go as planned. Taking a few minutes to reflect on what works well—and what needs tweaking—can make all the difference for your family. The following suggestions will get you started on a successful beginning to your day:

- Get up five minutes earlier to take a little time in the bathroom by yourself.

- Anticipate the timing to greet your child before he is fussy.

- Stay realistic about how much time you really need before you have to leave home, so that late experiences are minimized.

- Set up your morning coffee routine with mug ready the night before.

- Keep plenty of healthy grab-it-on-the-go breakfast options ready.

- Lay out clothes for yourself, so you don't need to find them when your child wakes up and needs you.

- Choose your child's clothes and set out needed books and materials the night before.

- Offer puzzles and books to keep your child occupied while you straighten up.

- Keep toothbrushes in a bathroom near the kitchen to streamline the routine.

- Play soothing music to boost the morning mood.

The key to an easier start is to set up a morning routine that works. Necessary activities should be fun for everyone—or at least doable! The person who may need to adjust most, of course, is you. You may need to go to bed earlier, which acts as a domino effect for revisiting evening routines. When things do not work, make adjustments right away.

Allowing Imperfection

Saturday morning shrieks and laughter wake me up from sleep. I roll out of bed to find my five-year-old sitting on the floor in the midst of cereal, and my four-year-old pouring milk. He smiles and says, "Look, Daddy! I can do it myself!" Option one is to scrape the cobwebs from my sleepy brain and gripe, "I told you to come get me before you came downstairs." But I know there are only fourteen more summers before these cute fellows head into the big world. So I say, "Yes, sir. You are getting so big! Let's clean this up together." Next week, I'll get to the kitchen first.

It takes a gargantuan amount of energy to stay patient when your children's needs conflict with your own. It may seem like you'll never have enough sleep and that parenting will last forever. But you have only a limited time to make your mark. So as you pour your coffee or juice, congratulate yourself on finding your cool—and keeping the end goal in mind.

We all know the feeling of needing a break, checking out emotionally instead of checking in, or wishing we could change our attitudes. It's easy to feel discouraged, and it takes time and patience to put new plans in place. Just as you don't expect perfection of yourself, be patient and give your children time to gain skills. When you feel frustrated or wish your children would "just grow up," remember that they learn—just like you do—step by step. They need your cheering and encouragement so that they feel good about their efforts.

Some of us spend a lifetime sorting out who we are from what we do. Once learned, perfectionism is a lens that can affect your vision for years to come. The messages we pick up shape the way we see ourselves and others. Your children are vulnerable to your words. If you force your children to be perfectionistic by criticizing, this can feel devastating. Negative words instill a basic hesitancy and insecurity at the core of a child's inner self. However, words of affirmation take root in a child's spirit and foster freedom to try new things and to grow.

If you have experienced criticism in the past, replace those negative messages with new affirmations. Look in the mirror and say, "This is going to be okay. You are enough. You have what it takes to accomplish this day. You can do this." Start by showing kindness and compassion for your own experience.

If you can embrace a deep sense of gratitude for the opportunity to be alive and present in each day, to accept your own unique perspectives, feelings, and gifts, then you can gain strength. You may wrestle briefly with the struggles but choose to grow. Celebrate the journey set before you. Nourish yourself with care so that you can grow fully into all you were meant to be.

In the same way, let your children know that they are enough for you. When they try to help and the results aren't perfect, let it go. When they make a mistake, forgive. When they need patience, show grace. When things are not going well, give a hug. Through your response, they can see that your love never wavers. They can know you are here for the long haul, ready to teach and guide, and that you will stay in their corner to cheer them on. All children need this pillar of strength behind them.

> Don't demand perfection. Cheer the effort that sorted the toys, rather than focus on a stray few that have been left behind. Focus on good habits that are developing.

You can't make life perfect, but stay sensitive to the way you come across. The way you speak, your body language, your tone of voice, and your facial expression all create meaning as much as the words you say. Becoming aware of yourself helps you understand how much your words have the power to encourage or discourage your children.

Children learn they are "just right" by the way you are patient and kind. You can't wait to talk with them and hear their ideas. You enjoy watching them work and play. You love being with them and love your time with them. You need to say these things out loud as well as show them in your actions. We all want to know that we are valued and honored for who we are. It helps to consider the messages we give.

- **Focus on internal character qualities rather than on physical attributes.**
  The stress to conform to physical standards puts children in jeopardy of self-doubt. Focus comments on inner traits, such as kindness, caring, effort, and a sense of humor.

- **Monitor words that reveal attitudes.** Children are sensitive to our ideas. If they hear you demean someone else, they know you have the capability to feel the same way about them. If they hear you put them down, the labels stick like glue and are difficult to pull out of their memories. If you had critical parents, this tendency is something you need to monitor. Remember the old adage, "If you can't say something kind, don't say anything at all."

- **Focus on what matters.** Compliment for what went well instead of focusing on what went wrong. Rather than focusing on your child's mistake, say, "You are making so much progress!" "You worked so hard," "You were such a big help," or "You are learning how to do it."

- **Don't cry over spilled milk.** When mishaps occur, be reassuring, even if there's a mess. It's okay to say, "I know you'll be more careful next time." It also is important to acknowledge the child's feelings. "I am so sorry the milk spilled. I know you feel bad. It's okay. We can clean it up together." Not only will this reassure your child, but it will help you stay calm, as well.

- **Nurture the spirit.** Words of encouragement will foster the traits you hope for in yourself and in your children: "You handled that upset so well. I am so thankful for all the ways you are growing." Give a blessing to yourself and to your child. Children long for our reassurance. Cheerful words can turn around a gloomy moment, and a spirit of thankfulness can soften a child's heart.

Freedom from perfection and fear will come when you ignore the pressures and images of the perfect mother or father and become the person of your own heart—fully present and growing in love with patience for yourself and others. Once you know how good this acceptance feels, you can pass on it to your children. Once they know how good this feels, they can give this gift to their own children one day—and to others in their lives. They will become caring and thoughtful teens, because the roots of empathy and respect will have grown strong and deep during their childhood years.

Embracing Your Personal Style

What works for your family is best for your family. I've talked to other women who have recently had babies, and they do things differently than I do. They may not cosleep, or they may schedule feedings instead of being on demand. In the end, it's not about what other people think is right or wrong. It's what helps your family bond and adapt the best—and get the most sleep!

Every child needs to be able to trust that the adult will be consistent. What comes next? Does the routine feel familiar? Children will relax and gain confidence when they can trust what is happening.

The key to getting it right as a parent is to take into account our own needs and lifestyle. If you are a night owl, your child may go to bed later than if you were an early-to-bed type. If you are a creative spirit instead of an organizer, those toys strewn on the carpet may not seem like an issue. If you like things in a line, put away, or tidy, then you will keep a greater sense of order. It is not the minor details that matter to your child's sense of security but the consistency of your approach and routine.

You are the center of your child's sense of security. When baby is hungry, he will learn to count on what happens next. If he knows you will come quickly when you hear him, he will cry less and be easier to soothe. Instead of becoming anxious, he gets to know your sounds and regular patterns. He understands when he is changed, tucked in his jacket, and buckled in the car seat that he is going to Grandma's house or to the store. When he finds you are consistent, he chills out and happily goes along with your plans.

Older children also become accustomed to your way of doing things. We each have a special manner of relating and specific habits of living. You may be a take-along kind of parent and feel comfortable bringing your child with you when you are running errands. Or you may prefer to leave your child with someone when you go out. The way you laugh, the conversations you enjoy, and even the way you move and talk are unique.

Embracing your own personal style can help you keep a sense of balance and joy. What matters most is the warm, centered responsiveness you bring to your interactions that respects and honors your child's needs in each moment.

Becoming mindful of the effects of routines and activities can help you become more aware of what is happening as children respond. It will pay off to consider what works best for you and then aim to establish and keep a regular pattern. Your goal is to better understand how your consistency can positively influence your children's reactions.

- **Keep a spiral notebook or a calendar system.** This easy-to-find resource can help you manage your appointments, keep track of needed items, and update your to-do list.

- **Plan a daily schedule in blocks of time.** Note what works well and what needs to be adjusted. Over a few weeks, you will arrive at a basic schedule that best suits your child and your needs.

- **Write down sweet and funny moments.** You will want to record new words or something funny that was said. Keep track of growth, milestones, first steps, and first days of school. You are keeping a record of memories for your family and for your child.

- **Record items for attention.** Perhaps you notice something that is not working well. Jot it down as a reminder to consider alternative approaches or solutions. Your goal is to find out what works.

- **Make habits stick.** Put your keys in the same place every time. At the end of a phone conversation, return the phone to a specific place in the room. When mail comes, take out the bills immediately and put them in a ziplock bag or a basket that contains nothing else. When you want to save a receipt, put it immediately into a container marked for that purpose. According to the 2004 article "Clean Freaks" published by *Newsweek,* the average American spends between fifteen minutes to an hour or more a day looking for what we cannot find. How much better to avoid frustration and spend that time with the ones we love.

- **Create special memories.** Your family traditions may be waffles for breakfast on Sundays or a particular dish for New Year's Eve dinner. You may sing a special song at a meal or make a silly rhyme for getting in the car. Choose activities that make you truly happy. Enjoy these moments as they occur.

Children love to remember and to look forward to things they can count on. It gives them a sense of stability, predictability, and belonging to talk about the day's events. Even before children can talk, the sound of your voice talking about what you did together reassures them. Sharing what you plan to do tomorrow when children go to bed can help them sleep happily with anticipation for what will come. When you establish these kinds of connections through routines and traditions, you make parenting work for you.

Each day brings a fresh opportunity to create the kinds of relationships with your children that will prepare them for the teen years ahead—and that will nurture a life of trust and lasting connections with others. These relationships are the heart of parenting and form the center of a meaningful and fulfilling journey of love. Children inspire us to become our best selves. As you aim for the future, you can parent with confidence, knowing you are building a strong foundation that will last.

> As author Elizabeth Stone says, "Making the decision to have a child—it's momentous. It is to decide forever to have your heart go walking outside your body." You anticipate the love, but you don't really know until your baby gazes at you with absolute trust. Then you know you will do anything at all to live up to his belief in you.

Parenting can inspire you with a fresh vision and give you the opportunity to renew empathy and kindness toward yourself and others.

- **Be positive.** Children are watching all of the time. They will do what they see. They catch your tone of voice and expressions. What you give to them in positive energy and sensitive words will come back to you in your children's voice and behavior. They will adopt your behavior, values, and attitudes.

- **Be responsive.** Mirror children's body language. Make conversation reciprocal as you talk about your day. Keep getting to know your child. Ask yourself, "What can I do to comfort, encourage, and build my child's security and confidence?" "What does my child need from me right now?"

- **Plan realistic time expectations.** Add five minutes to your timetable for each additional person when you need to go somewhere or get something done. If you are not sure how long you need, use a timer to find out. That will give you a true picture, so that you can make adjustments next time.

- **Respond later.** When someone invites you to do something, say, "Thanks for asking. Let me have some time to think about it, and I will get back to you." Take time to weigh your options.

- **Take mini-breaks to fuel your mind, body, and spirit.** Enjoy a few deep breaths. Stretch. Pray. Look outside your window and take in the changing seasons or beautiful day to keep yourself centered.

- **Don't compare.** All of us have different temperaments, different ways of living, and different needs. It may look like someone else has it all together, but every parent is working hard to make things happen. Push away inner doubts and focus only on the people and things that inspire you to feel and be positive about all you are doing. Borrow creative ideas from others—only if those work for you.

CHAPTER 2
CONNECTING
WITH LOVE

Nurturing the Connection Zone

Someone told me there were only 2,000 days between birth and kindergarten. That gave me the perspective I needed. Best advice? Don't wait until your child is fussy to step in. Best investment ever? Enjoy bedtime routines, especially as your child gets older. The snuggling, reading, and talking make the best time of the day.

Your children long to feel that you are engaged and focused on them. They need your undivided attention. A magic zone of connection happens when you put distractions aside and really tune in to your child. You might enjoy silly laughter with funny faces and songs. You might spend time together sharing physical closeness. The most important ingredient is your emotional presence.

Because your baby senses your every move, she seems almost intuitive about your feelings. Babies know if we are fully present by the way we hold and look at them. This incredible connection never changes. Your toddler will pick up on your excitement. She will tune in to your slightest change of expression. Toddlers watch their caregivers' faces to gauge their safety and to check on their response or to look for their approval. Preschoolers know when a parent is upset just by a glance. Even adult children watch their parents' faces to see if they feel happy, anxious, or worried.

Children depend on their parents or caregivers to nurture, feed, and soothe them. It takes time to learn children's unique patterns and needs, and as soon as you think you have everything figured out, it seems like their internal clock shifts. A toddler who has slept through the night regularly starts waking up. A three-year-old with a sunny disposition has a meltdown. Parenting involves being responsive no matter what comes and understanding that every child is different.

> Every child needs a parent who cares and wants to spend time with him. Show your child how special she is to you each day. You are laying down a strong foundation of love that will last a lifetime.

When your baby fusses, you instinctively feel tense. After all, you want to do a good job. You may wonder if you are doing the right things. Sometimes you may worry about the judgment of others who are watching. Take a deep breath and relax. This moment of self-awareness can calm and center you, so that you can then work confidently to try different positions or ways of comforting and can attend to your baby's needs.

Some parents feel nurturing and needed at the thought of snuggling with a contented baby or child. Others may not be comfortable with this level of closeness. Perhaps what comes to mind is a sick toddler who sticks to you like glue while she has a fever and wet pajamas. Becoming aware of yourself and your responses can make all the difference. Because your child tunes into your emotions, you are the first person who needs to become calm when things shift or change. Being able to focus outward to your child and yet inward to yourself can help you become more sensitive as you navigate both your child's needs and your own.

Children are learning to recognize and respond to their own needs. An infant may be upset after his mother drives away—she needs reassurance and distraction with a toy or song. A toddler may still be excited after Grandma leaves. She needs help to build a bridge between the excitement of packing bags into the car and the quiet evening routines to come. Children need assistance with the transition between states of calm and activity.

You can help your child recognize the physical signs for her needs: "You are yawning! Your yawn says you are sleepy. Are you sleepy? It feels good to curl up with a book for some quiet time when you are sleepy." "You look hot and sweaty. Would you like to come inside for a drink of water and a rest?" "You look bored. Let's take a bike ride together and enjoy the afternoon sun." Trust the cues you see to develop an overall picture of what is happening. Then, help your child become sensitive to and responsive to her body's cues.

Children who are aware of themselves also become good at reading others. They become the ones who will say, "May I help you? That looks heavy," when they see someone struggling to carry a heavy bag. They will comfort a friend in school and feel sympathetic to their siblings at home. This kind of emotional intelligence is an asset in every area of life.

When you think about your goals, dreams, and desires for your child, set aside worry when things don't happen exactly as you want them, and take it easy when it feels like you have taken two steps forward and three steps back. Be patient with yourself and with your child. Keep focused on the progress that you and your child are making.

A wonderful side effect of being a parent is that you are inspired to grow as a human being. You may become more thoughtful about the legacy you will leave. You know you need to prepare your child for the teen years and for life ahead. Realizing how quickly children grow up can help you keep your perspective. Focus on the quality of the connection you are creating. This essential bond sets the pattern for security and happiness and creates a lasting relationship of trust and love.

> Remember, children have feelings, too. We want to treat them as well or better than we treat other people for whom we are not responsible. Having this perspective, we can keep their best interests in mind.

Bonding with a Purpose

After all the sleepless nights, the food on my shirt, the crackers and cereal stuck under the car seats, the plastic toys I have to remove from the tub before my shower, the bazillionth diaper I've changed, and the loads of laundry, I find myself staring down at my not-so-young daughter who is about to start kindergarten. I wish I had those first years back. Have I done enough? Is she prepared to start the road ahead? Can I survive watching her leave in the morning—knowing my life will be forever changed? I wish I had pictured this day more and treasured the achingly precious moments every step of the way. As I watch her sleep, I wish I could slow down the clock.

Through a bonding touch at birth to shared gazing and cooing in infancy, morning snuggles with toddlers, and cozy lap time for young children, a deep sense of security and strength takes root. Home is the place where we feel safe and accepted in a circle of understanding and unconditional love.

Warm and responsive relationships in the first five years of life actually predict success in school and act as a protective factor when life brings challenges. The first three years are critical for the development of language, cognitive growth, and social-emotional competence. From age four to age eight, increasing knowledge and understanding relies on the critical foundations of the first three years. You aren't simply caring for your children—you are wiring their brains for the future and nourishing their spirit of creativity, motivation, and excitement to learn.

How does a baby experience the nurturing power of connection? An infant's world is a kaleidoscope of sensations. She feels the calm of your soothing and secure touch. She relaxes with your comforting warmth and gentle rocking and patting. She orients toward your face, seeking the responsive back-and-forth interactions that make her feel happy and that introduce her to the amazing world of language and communication. Your baby depends on you to initiate and to respond to her through this shared connection.

In the book *Thirty Million Words: Building a Child's Brain,* author Dana Suskind makes it simple: "Tune in. Talk more. Take turns." As you share smiles, mimic expressions, and respond to your baby's vocalizations, you give your child a gift that will pay off now and in the future with the ability to communicate, express feelings, self-regulate, and grow in healthy ways. Neuroscience shows us that parents and caregivers have tremendous influence to maximize children's potential, not only through words alone but also through warm responsiveness and healthy relationship patterns.

Throughout the day, there are specific strategies that can help you tune in and see what your child needs from you—something that will make you feel better, too.

- **Smile!** Children scan caregivers' faces for reassurance. Your emotional connection directly increases your child's relaxation and sense of security.

- **Spend private time together.** Connect at your child's eye level to create a caring bridge of focused attention.

- **Pay attention to cues.** "You seem extra quiet this morning. Did something make you feel sad?" Observe your child's body language to help you stay responsive. Verbalize what you see to help your child link physical and emotional sensations to words that can express her feelings.

- **Stay tuned in to experiences.** Describe physical sensations to promote your child's awareness. "Doesn't the water feel warm and slippery?" "Is your tummy saying you are hungry?" "Brrr. It's cold. Let's put on a sweater to keep you warm."

- **Be your child's first teacher.** Share your love and enjoyment of the world around you. "Listen to the birds. Do you see the robins?" Children are constantly learning, and you can light up their world with shared curiosity and interesting conversation.

- **Model nurturing behaviors.** Take time to cuddle and give hugs throughout the day. Try an arm tickle, a hand squeeze, or stroking your child's hair. Draw patterns lightly on the skin, or give a gentle massage on the forearm or back when you are near. Take a few moments to massage your baby's feet and legs after diapering, as you coo and soothe. The singsong language adults use with young children is often called *motherese* or *parentese*—speaking in a high voice and stretching out vowels with expressive tones. This gentle but exaggerated speech boosts a baby's language acquisition. Patricia Kuhl, coauthor of *The Scientist in the Crib: What Early Learning Tells Us about the Mind,* says that babies' brains are mapping the sounds they hear.

- **Assist during transitions.** Remain sensitive to the need for soothing when your child must transition from one activity to another. Assist your child with the shift between arousal and calm through predictable patterns in routines, words, and actions, so that she feels reassured and comfortable.

Sometimes an older child may want to tell you something important, but you may be distracted. Instead of mumbling, "Hmmm," it's better to get on the child's eye level and give her your full attention: "I am so glad you told me." "I can see how much you care about that!" Your words will hit their mark because you have taken time to make eye contact and really listen. You will have shown your child that you want to connect.

There will be special events and uncommon memories to come, but shared day-to-day moments are the stuff life is made of. Pulling a high chair near while you prepare food, talking while you fold clothes, brushing your teeth together, or giggling together at bedtime reveal the extraordinary connections found in common moments. Come alongside your child and keep her near as you live and work, sheltering her in the circle of your presence. These daily patterns of intimate connection nurture and secure a lasting bond.

On the days when this together time feels endless and you long for time alone, remind yourself that early close and warm connections over these days and weeks will secure a lasting anchor of confidence for your child. Through patient guidance and care, your child will gradually internalize growing her independence and skill. As she grows into the toddler years, she'll be able to play alone for longer periods and one day will surprise you by spending a morning in contented, self-directed play. During the early years, it can seem like the needs are incessant and you will never get a break. Be certain that these moments matter, and your love, care, and patience are truly gifts that will keep on giving for the rest of your child's life.

> When talking with your child, get down at her eye level and talk softly. Tune in to body language, tone of voice, and facial expression. Really listen.

Activating Attachment

My wife and I got hit with a double dose of love when we had twins. We were in awe. All we could think was, "They are so tiny. How are we going to do this?" Their facial expressions were our daily entertainment. Get ready for lots of laughter and noise, big hugs, and so many joys. Parenting truly is priceless.

Children are wired for attachment—the powerful and lasting bond between a child and parent. Cooing, comforting, and rocking all light up baby's brain and your own with oxytocin, a hormone released by the pituitary gland. Oxytocin is called the "tend and befriend" hormone, as it increases your sense of well-being when you are close to someone you love.

Oxytocin sets off a chain of instructions to the brain. The biochemical rush increases optimism, self-esteem, and mood. During labor and childbirth, oxytocin assists the body with contractions. It is transferred to the newborn through breast milk and also is released by the baby's brain during skin-to-skin contact. This initial bonding is so important to a baby as well as to the parents.

Even anticipation of being close to someone you love boosts your sense of happiness. A touch, laugh, or smile can set off a reaction of positive brain patterns that enhances your immune system, makes you think more clearly, and nurtures your emotional health. A hug is more than a way of showing affection or a feel-good moment. It gives a lasting benefit to the child who receives it and to the one who gives it. Safe and comforting touch throughout childhood makes both you and your child healthier.

One of the most important connections happens during sleep and feeding routines. When your baby is anxious or crying, she needs your soothing and comfort so that she comes to associate her physical needs with relaxation rather than with anxiety. According to researchers Jodi Mendell et al. and Lauren Philbrook et al., children who are soothed while falling asleep have fewer sleep-adjustment issues both right away and in the future. The following guidelines are essential for baby—and will continue to be needed as your child gets older.

- **Develop a consistent sleep routine.** Bed and nap times should be happy, safe, and secure. Begin with your baby to develop a consistent pattern and sequence. Give a warm bath, enjoy snuggle time, and follow with gentle rocking. Tucking-in time, after your baby has been fed, bathed, and dressed in clean pajamas, is the perfect time to sing familiar songs, look at picture books, and relax. This routine sets the pattern for bedtime that will last through the school-age years.

- **Read books.** The American Academy of Pediatrics recommends that parents read aloud to babies beginning at birth. The sound of your voice, the patterns of inflection, and rhythm of words build needed language connections in the brain. Reading at bedtime throughout childhood can instill a lasting love of books and creates a happy shared tradition.

- **Sleep safely.** Be sure to follow your pediatrician's guidelines and place your baby to sleep on her back without blankets, crib bumpers, or other soft objects in the crib. At first, swaddle your infant, and as she gets bigger, dress her in a warm sleeper over pajamas if you live in a cool climate. When your baby can roll over in both directions, she may choose to sleep on her tummy. As children get older, respect their preferences for comfort.

- **Spend time together.** "Baby wearing" provides additional soothing and bonding during the day. Ring slings and Moby-type wraps provide hammock-style support that secures your newborn to your chest, while distributing the weight. Many brands offer carriers that provide comfortable options as baby gets bigger. Be sure to follow all safety directions.

Children who find a secure home base of trust and feel attachment with their parents receive an incredible payoff with lasting rewards. According to researchers Lee Raby et al. and Richard Bowlby, these children enjoy greater sensitivity and empathy for themselves and others. They have more self-confidence and self-esteem. They have fewer behavior problems and are more adaptable in new situations. They develop closer friendships and get along better in school. Science tells us that what we do now is an investment that matters! Most importantly, the bond that we nurture today lays the foundation for the kind of relationships our children will have with us and others in the years to come.

Securing Your Relationship Foundation

I want to be patient, polite, and forgiving because that is how I want each of my children to behave toward one another. When I am having a hard day, everyone is having a hard day, so I remind myself that what I am doing matters. I am shaping the way my children view themselves.

When children feel close to us, they long to be like us and to please us. Children who feel connected typically listen better, tune in, and want to cooperate. They internalize the values of the ones they admire and who make them feel safe. We need to do everything within our power to keep this sacred connection intact.

Children need a zone of safety and acceptance every day. They long to feel and stay close to their parents and caregivers. When your child comes to you and wants to connect, she will look to see if your face lights up and if you will welcome her to stay near. Your child wants to feel your favor and affection. The following can help you create a rewarding relationship zone with your child each day:

- Curling up to read a book

- Talking over dinner

- Stopping with hug to say, "I'm glad you're here."

- Sharing secrets at bedtime

- Laughing or telling jokes together

- Using private pet names

- Having a secret handshake or high-five

- Treasuring unique butterfly kisses or nose rubs

- Taking time to let your child help or plan

- Teaching a new skill

- Saying an affirmation, such as, "I love to listen to you playing with your friend."

- Having a special one-on-one date

- Dancing together

> Find multiple ways to connect with your child. Help her to discover her strengths, uniqueness, and special gifts by calling attention to them.

Your connection is your child's anchor. Think about the way you feel when you are with someone you love: accepted, peaceful, and happy. For those of us who are pet lovers, curling up with a cat or dog actually lowers blood pressure and boosts the immune system. The same is true for happy relationships at home.

According to the Centers for Disease Control, early positive relationships with Mom and Dad actually protect children from health problems and boost their physical health outcomes throughout life. Protection from stress and warm security leads to greater well-being and mental health. When we truly listen, see life through children's eyes, and cheer them on with gentleness and care, that close bond will set them on a course toward a healthy and happy life.

Using Strategies to Soothe

My doorbell rang. The dog threw up a sock. My two children were shoving each other, and one ran through the wet mess. I pulled off my toddler's socks, gave out hugs, put on music, spread out a blanket, and passed out juice pops. They took the bait and plopped down on the floor with juice pops in hand. Two seconds later, my husband's parents walked in. You have to know as a parent, there are going to be a lot of close calls. Chaos is just a minute away.

Knowing how to calm down a situation—or a child or yourself—is an essential skill of parenting. There are ways to make things easier, such as preparing ahead, understanding your child's limits, and keeping child-friendly materials on hand to distract and engage. Sometimes you can give a hug or guide your child to a safe place to recover from an upset. But other times, it can be a challenge to deal with stress, anxiety, or anger.

Using effective strategies beginning in infancy sets the pattern that can help older children refocus and settle down more quickly. Knowing how your child responds best and sharing these details with others involved in her care can help ensure that routines stay consistent. Below are some good options for soothing:

- **Use rhythmic movement.** Rub your child's arms, legs, or back gently while nursing or feeding her. Walk or sway rhythmically with soft reassurance or shushing. Gentle rocking, singing, humming, and quiet words are calming for children.

- **Practice soothing touch.** Keep a hand securely on your baby's tummy while diapering or bathing her. Massaging a toddler's shoulders can help her relax. You can rub feet, hold hands, and trace patterns on the arms of older children. Safe, comforting touch is essential.

- **Provide extended bath rituals.** Swaddle or wrap your baby securely with a light blanket or soft towel after bathing her. Try infant massage with natural hypoallergenic, fragrance-free oil or another gentle, doctor-approved, unscented lotion. Older children calm more easily with a quiet bath transition. Give time to play and relax in the water. Stay near, and use safe cleansing products.

- **Honor sensory needs.** Stay responsive to your child's unique reactions to light, sound, and textures. Some children develop an aversion to certain foods (especially those that are slimy, grainy, or hairy) and other materials such as cotton balls; playdough; or the feel of certain sheets, blankets, or clothing.

- **Calm with sound.** Use a sound machine to mimic the noises of a mother's womb, the rain, or ocean waves. Sound apps on your smart phone can be used when traveling in the car. Using sound as a cue for sleep works effectively for toddlers, as well. Older children also fall asleep peacefully with nature sounds and gentle lullabies.

With your children, you set the emotional thermostat. When you are gentle in helping your toddler get dressed, she is likely to stay calm during the process. If you are patient with your three-year-old when she is slow to finish her dinner, she can focus on getting done without a fuss. When you comfort your six-year-old with caring words and a hug when she is upset, she is better able to move forward. This universal need for support does not change as children grow older.

Often a tired child simply needs a hug, just as you would. When a child is frustrated, you can see how quickly reassurance helps her move forward. This perspective can guide your words and actions. The goal is to treat children in the way you want to be treated, with honor and respect for their spirits as well as their bodies.

When you see things through your child's eyes, you can be more responsive to her needs. Children often need guidance while they figure out what they feel and need support while they decide what to do. Thinking about what would be most helpful to them is the key to success.

> It pays to take a deep breath and think twice, so that you proceed gently. Ask yourself, "Would I want someone to do that to me? How would I feel?" Children will treat us the way we treat them.

Getting Enough Sleep

Parents often read the books, freak about sleep training, and compare their baby with other babies. I decided to do what worked for my baby. I followed his lead, and after a couple of months he slept by himself. I listened to all the things my friends were trying. But in the end, I just did what he needed. He naps twice a day and sleeps through the night. It took a little time, but it was worth taking it as it came.

Sleep is one of the most important prerequisites for happy and well-adjusted parents and children. Sleep ranks at the top of most people's priorities, along with health and exercise. When you are well-rested, things go much better. You will have the energy to think clearly and to nurture your children with patience. When children are rested, they will be more flexible and will respond with positive emotions. There will be fewer cranky moments for all.

You may know at least one family who puts their baby to bed with a dozen pacifiers—one in every corner and spread out around the crib—so that in case baby wakes up, she can find a "paci" without needing to call for help. Whether you call it a "binky," "nukie," or "suessy," some parents find them indispensable. Other parents can't get their baby to take one—no matter how hard they try. This effort points out how desperate parents are for sleep.

The most important factor in happy sleeping is to protect routines and spaces as comforting and peaceful. Some methods that use a philosophy of gentle support and nurture include *The Attachment Parenting Book: A Commonsense Guide to Understanding and Nurturing Your Baby* by William Sears and Martha Sears, *The Happiest Baby on the Block* by Harvey Karp, and *Twelve Hours' Sleep by Twelve Weeks Old* by Suzy Giordano. Importantly, these approaches honor the need of every child for security and advocate responsive soothing rather than letting a baby cry. Parents anticipate and respond to children's needs in consistent ways.

There are many reasons to comfort your baby rather than let her cry without assistance:

- Babies are still developing their nervous systems and need assistance with soothing. This is called *coregulation*, as your infant will match her breathing and sense of calm to your own.

- Crying increases rather than decreases anxiety. You don't want the baby to associate sleep with anxiety.

- Crying makes the bed a place of struggle instead of comfort. Children learn to comfort themselves when they know how being comforted feels.

- Your baby may fall asleep out of exhaustion, but then you have missed an opportunity to bond and connect. This is the time to set healthy patterns. Falling asleep upset and exhausted goes against the goal of establishing soothing and nurturing sleep practices. Sensitive and responsive care shows the baby how to honor her needs.

- By being available to your baby, you foster trust, intimacy, and empathy.

- A struggle-free sleep pattern set in infancy lasts into the toddler years and beyond.

- Letting your baby cry and not saying anything about it to others in the home teaches older children not to care when their sibling is distressed. If the parent models disinterest in the baby's distress, it should be no surprise when children then disconnect from their sibling's distress.

When you help your infant learn to settle and soothe, you set the internal blueprint for needed self-care and for healthy future sleep patterns. Older children whose needs have been met at bedtime will associate going to sleep with a sense of security, pleasure, and comfort. The practice of responsive nurturing results in a lifetime of benefits in healthy sleep habits.

Once you know your older infant can sleep for longer stretches, you can enter quietly at night to settle and soothe without talking or making noise. It can help to go in before baby fully wakes up to pat her gently and support her return to sleep. With toddlers and preschoolers, you may need to soothe after a dream; help with a wet bed; or give occasional quiet, gentle support in the night. The waking will soon pass when you keep routines consistent and respond with reassurance. The key is to keep yourself calm.

Nurture consistent sleep routines. Bedtime is the most intimate time of day to talk about what happened at home or school, to share secrets and stories, and to spend precious time together. Start early enough to include backrubs and nighttime stories. Tucking-in routines are a needed source of reassurance and connection. Researchers Yvonne Kelly, John Kelly, and Amanda Sacker have found that this investment will spill over into the next morning's behavior and activities. The consistent ritual will pay off in a more rested child and better behavior over time.

The research by Max Hirshkowitz et al. for the National Sleep Foundation provides some helpful guidelines regarding just how much sleep children need at different stages. Keep in mind that these numbers reflect total sleep hours in a twenty-four–hour period. If your child naps, you will need to take that into account when you add up sleep hours.

- Newborns (birth to three months): 14–17 hours

- Infants (four to eleven months): 12–15 hours

- Toddlers (one to two years): 11–14 hours

A nap usually puts everything in better perspective. Parents are often sleep deprived. Make it a priority to go to bed sooner at night, so that you have energy for the day.

- Preschoolers (three to five years): 10–13 hours

- School-age children (six to thirteen years): 9–11 hours

- Teenagers (fourteen to seventeen years): 8–10 hours

Set a new goal to be rested and fresh each day. Turn back the evening schedule so that the adults in your home get enough sleep. The goal is not perfection but growth toward optimal health. When you see your children becoming tired or lethargic, take a stretch break, a music break, or a brain break. Encourage quiet time for older children, and plan needed rest for younger children. You can turn things around and instill a fresh spirit of energy by helping everyone get some sleep.

Having Fun with Daily Transitions

Every time we are running late and need to get in the car, my youngest daughter picks that very moment to throw a fit. She wants her favorite doll, which is inevitably buried in a pile of toys in the back of a closet and can't be found.

Moving from an activity to a meal or getting dressed to leave can increase stress. These transitions are the times that children struggle, get frustrated, and cry most often. During the moment that you most want to get going and are in a hurry, your child stalls. You may feel that a transition is about getting yourself and your family where you need to be. At the same time, the child may feel that this experience is about her and what she needs. Understanding this conflict ahead of time can help you turn transitions into better experiences—instead of challenging ones.

Transitions give you the opportunity to fill your child's emotional tank and center on what is happening. Your child may want to snuggle in your bed or on the couch for a while before starting daily activities. She may need a few minutes of support before you leave for work or may need extra time to figure out a knotted shoelace. At these moments, she will need your undivided attention.

What happens before a transition is as important as what happens during it. If you are leaving for work or the normal schedule has changed, stay sensitive to your child's need for reassurance. Plan time to boost security and ease stress when you know you need to shift to a new activity or situation.

- **Ensure daytime cuddle routines.** A five-minute cuddle time can save the moment or turn around a day.

- **Encourage transitional objects.** A treasured stuffed animal, blanket, or other "lovey" toy is a natural support for young children and can be tucked in to take along.

- **Try warm comforts.** A warming sock or gently heated pillow can relax the body and spirit. Be sure to test the temperature and follow safety information.

- **Share deep breathing and stretching activities.** With your children, touch the floor, reach for the ceiling with climbing hand motions, or extend your arms wide. Breathing and stretching can calm everyone down. Finish with a hug.

- **Share silly words and phrases.** Familiar cues such as "skit, skat, skitteo" or "quicker than a jack rabbit" can make a game out of pulling off a shirt or changing clothes.

- **Have a "ready box."** Meltdowns often happen when needed items can't be found. Keep a few extra pairs of socks, underwear or diapers, a brush and hairbands, and other frequently needed items where you can grab them on the go. Your ready box really will save the day.

- **Create a comfort station.** A soft bean bag, indoor tent, or open cardboard box with pillows can provide a happy quiet place where your child can chill. Some children enjoy a weighted sensory blanket, as the pressure and texture soothe stress.

- **Keep positive meal and diapering or bathroom routines.** Bond with shared conversation and through offering your full attention. These activities should be happy and fun—without pressure or stress.

Transitions are a perfect time to have fun. Singing a song, telling stories, focusing on a tickle or silly joke while dressing a child can contribute to success. Counting steps while walking out to the car can refocus attention. What seems like a chore can be a perfect time for bonding. Even when you only have a moment, connecting through smiles and laughter can make all the difference in how things turn out.

When we see families having fun, it is important to know that they make it happen. A mom said, "My husband and I are raising our four kids to have fun, laugh a lot, share their

> Children love to know that they bring us joy and pleasure. Lighten up and have fun together. Shared laughter increases optimism and creates positive solutions to what otherwise might feel like a challenge.

feelings, and give more than they receive. We want them to love life, so we are living in the moment to enjoy them." Let your children know that you can make life happen rather than let it happen to you. This is a mindset that can change everything.

Setting Priorities

Wesley started preschool today. He got to the classroom and said, "Bye, Mom. See ya!" Isn't he supposed to be a little sad? They grow up way too fast. I can never believe how quickly the little ones change.

Many parents grow with their children. Their childhood becomes our second childhood as we fly down the slide at the park or play hide-and-go-seek with them. If you live in a rural area, a trip to a pumpkin patch for cider and donuts may revive a happy tradition from your past. In the city, weekend festivals and art fairs may become a family affair. Pass forward your fond memories and create new ways of celebrating together.

For some of us, our children's childhood can remind us of difficult challenges, such as struggling to finish or find homework, handling our parents' divorce, or making a long-distance move. Make the most of every opportunity to create a world of security and strength, yet know that not all things are within your control.

On Sunday night, your child may come running to say, "Oh, by the way, I have to write a report on our state and it has to be on poster board." You realize that you used the last of the poster board yesterday as a drop cloth while painting a table and the poster board is now crumpled in the trash. What seems stressful today will make a funny story when you tell it to a friend. Even in the most organized households with the most caring of parents, crazy moments will come. When your child needs a random item that is missing, it helps to stay flexible and make do with whatever you have on hand.

Even when you do plan ahead and have a routine that works, things can go awry. A tired child can have a tantrum for no apparent reason or become fixated on wearing clothes that don't fit or are in the wash. Of course, this may seem to happen only when you need to be somewhere in a hurry. It's as if there is a magic button that alerts your child to your need to get going and spurs her to do the opposite.

In times like these, priorities matter. So what if the shirt and pants do not match? Your child's clothing is not a reflection of your parenting skills. You can turn this time of frustration into a nonevent and replace it with positive conversation. Keep calm—and move on. The more you practice, the better you will get at being flexible and finding the best solutions that can turn frustrating experiences into positive memories.

If you want to take your child out, but she is tired and wants to snuggle, let the trip go. If you plan an elaborate dinner but your child needs attention, go with a simple meal. If you schedule a fun art activity but your child wants to keep playing in the fort, cheer her on. If you want to read, but she is wiggly, take a dance break.

> In the middle of something that is not working, move on to something else. Destress yourself. Be willing to stay flexible and switch directions quickly when you see your child is unable to focus or needs a break.

Knowing how to let go, to turn your attention forward, and to be flexible are key skills of parenting. The truth is, solutions for challenges are often right within your sight, if you can only look up and see what is present. The "Serenity Prayer," attributed to theologian Reinhold Niebuhr, contains this truth for parents:

> *God, grant me the serenity to accept the things I cannot change,*
> *The courage to change the things I can,*
> *And the wisdom to know the difference.*

Bonding with an Adopted Child

> *We waited for nine years for our two boys, and they are the answer to our prayers. Because of their early insecure living situation, we try to encourage them every day with consistency and love. We were expecting we would do a lot to change their lives, but they are the ones who have changed ours.*

If you have adopted an infant or younger child, there are many ways to establish and nurture a secure relationship. Preschool and school-aged children will feel your heart and understand they are loved and safe as you give them the gift of belonging and connectedness.

If you have adopted an older child, establish daily routines for bed, bath, and meals with special songs and consistent expectations. The structure and predictability along with love and patience will build trust. Reassure your child every day of your love, both verbally and with hugs.

> From the beginning, build trust. As children get older, let them know—often and in many ways—that you trust their judgment. Create many opportunities for connection, competence, and closeness.

As you bond with your child, the guidance from this book will help you become a more resilient and responsive parent, able to share your strengths and love in the most powerful ways. These skills for behavior guidance will help you set consistent limits, communicate expectations, and meet your child's emotional needs. Importantly, strengthening your own sense of purpose and well-being will assist you in being a strong and healthy role model to your child.

The following practices will help you focus on your own growth as you honor and affirm your child's unique identity and sense of self.

- Record your child's new words, milestones, and experiences. Write about how much you love her and how precious this time is for you. Later on, this record will become a treasured reminder of your early connection.

- Keep a growth journal for your own journey of discovery and wisdom. Record your reflections, insights, and ideas.

- Take many photos and create a memory book to document what your child has said or done. Make establishing secure and happy memories a priority.

- Read books with your child that tell the stories of other adopted children. (For a list of recommended children's books, see page 191.) Read books that explore other parents' journeys of adoption for your own discovery and growth.

- Revisit your child's unique story through words and pictures. She will feel the love and pride you share.

If you have adopted an older child, honor her memories of the past, her bonds with others before you, and previous experiences of attachment and identity. Learn all you can about her background, ethnicity, and history—and affirm her unique sense of self. Answer questions honestly, following the child's lead and showing sensitivity to her spirit and understanding.

Help each child to feel cherished for her differences and to feel special, affirmed, and appreciated for the qualities that are uniquely hers. Children want to know they are loved just as they are and that they can never lose your love, no matter what they do. Through a secure bond and safe connection, children learn that they are worthy. This essential bond sets the pattern for security and happiness that will remain strong.

Seek the support of adoption organizations that can provide you with practical advice and give you a place to share your experiences with others. Connect with other parents for support. Make it a goal to create a wider network of secure relationships for your child with other children, adults, and family members.

There are many helpful resources for children who are older adoptees, sibling adoptees, and children with special needs, as well as those who need specific social-emotional interventions. In addition, early childhood organizations can be helpful to you as you enter or expand your world of parenting in this special way.

You have opened your heart and home to this precious child, and she is entrusting you with her life. As you stay responsive to her needs and strengths, you will develop a bond of love and a level of wisdom and compassion that will change you—and your child—forever.

Nurture your children's strengths by building your own. Make a list of the qualities you want to develop in yourself and your children, and post it as a reminder. When you feel great about your own choices, you will bring a sense of confidence to your parenting.

> Think of the outcome you want to achieve. Are you trying to take care of an issue for the moment, or are you helping the child learn important life skills? Keep your eye on the goal.

Positive relationships and caring interactions will become the heart of your home and will instill in your children a solid anchor of strength and security. This takes time, patience, and understanding of children's deepest need for belonging and love. Through your emotional presence— fully focused—you will come to know and appreciate who they really are. Authentic connection is your most powerful influence. Show up and stay present. What your children need most is a secure and loving relationship with you.

CHAPTER 3
SETTING UP FOR SUCCESS

Making Decisions

When we moved and our girls shared a room for the first time, we put them to bed and told them, "Lie still and don't talk to each other." I was worried that they might get silly and not fall asleep. But when my wife and I heard them whispering to each other, we realized that we really didn't want to enforce the rule. So the next night, we told them, "As long as you go to sleep soon, that's okay." We really wanted them to grow up sharing happy memories and becoming close friends.

The challenge in setting up children for success is that you need to make some decisions ahead of time about what rules are nonnegotiable and in which aspects of parenting you want to stay flexible. At first, you may not be sure how you want to do things or what will work best for your child. It can be hard to know what to limit until after something becomes a problem.

The mother of a four-year-old said, "I gave my son too many choices, and now it's hard to get control back. Truthfully, I wish I had set secure boundaries when he was little, like not letting him climb into the fridge to look for food. Sometimes I let him, and other times I didn't. Now he keeps going in there, and I know it's my fault for letting it go on for so long. Once I gave him the option, it was hard to turn it around."

The mother of an eight-year old said, "We often just fall into what is easiest at the time. We say, 'Fine. You can go ahead and play at your friend's house.' Last week I told her she could not go out until she got her room cleaned up first. I guess it's just laziness on my part, but I don't want her to be upset or complain, so I give in."

The father of a five-year old said, "When we are out shopping, I am in the habit of getting my son a pack of gum or a toy car every time we go to the store. I tell myself that I need to stop doing it, but if I don't my son thinks I am upset or being mean. It's really confusing for kids. I totally get it."

Your first child may take a while to sleep through the night; yet, your second child may go to sleep like a charm. You may think there is a difference between the two in physical need or temperament. But often what is different is that you have figured out what works for you and your children—and you know better how to get a baby to sleep.

Intentional planning can help you set up for success right from the start and will alleviate many typical behavior issues. Perhaps you don't mind if your toddler pulls the cushions off of the sofa to jump on them, or if your preschooler explores the refrigerator to get something to eat. Parenting decisions aren't made based on a universal code of "what is right." Instead, decide based on what is right for your family. There will be times when you'll have to tell your children that you have changed your mind and why. However, it helps to pick ground rules wisely and know that what you choose is what you are willing to stick with and enforce.

Once you decide on specific boundaries, it is important to be clear and consistent about following through. For example, if you want the children to brush their teeth every night before bed, you should try not to skip a night. When a pattern of inconsistency starts, reorienting becomes difficult. Of course there will be exceptions, such as when you come home late and you don't want to wake up a sleepy child, or your child is ill. But overall, consistent patterns are best.

For example, why do some parents struggle to keep a young toddler in the high chair while he is eating? If the toddler only receives food while in the chair, and sitting and being buckled in are prerequisites, then the child will know this is the routine. However, if the child has been allowed to eat outside of the chair or if parents have been inconsistent, then it may take patience to reestablish the pattern.

Safety is essential and nonnegotiable. "The seatbelt goes on before the car is put in gear." "We are careful near a hot stove." "We step onto the mat in the bathroom when getting out of the tub, so that we don't slip." When children need reminders, simply say, "I need you to be safe."

Children also learn that some rules are family rules. You may not mind if your children stand up to eat or walk around with food. However, consider the kinds of social skills that will help them succeed. At school and in other places, children will need to sit while eating. When you back this up at home, children gain valuable skills that will make their lives easier. Your job is not only to get through the minute or the meal but also to prepare your child for the future.

> It is important to tell children why rules exist so that they have a framework of understanding. Once the groundwork is set, blaming it on the rules can help the child follow through: "Our rule is to wash hands before eating." "Our rule is to eat food at the table."

Each family will decide on a unique combination of rules based on their preference and style. However, you want to set expectations that will help your children respect the needs of others, as well as take good care of themselves. Choose rules you are willing to live by, too. Once you decide on the nonnegotiables, step up and hold those limits. Set secure boundaries when children are little, and give them increasing freedom as they show increasing responsibility.

Taking Time to Teach

I tell my children, "Only take out what you can put away with a happy heart." But when they play at their friends' house, their parents don't care at all if toys get picked up right away. I really want my children to be appreciative and respectful of their things and to be responsible.

Young children's interest and energy will expand to fill every option available to them as they taste, touch, explore, and interact with the environment. This is why you should set limits on the cautious side at first, until you know what works best. Once you set the precedent that boundaries are wide and all objects and places are within touching limits, this expectation will be difficult to retract. For example, if you let baby play with items from Mommy's purse, he doesn't learn that these are her belongings. He thinks they are his toys. When you bring along a rattle for baby and keep it in a separate bag, he learns that Mommy's things belong to her.

Unless you intend for a child to continue to do an action, don't let him do it the first time. For example, don't let your toddler play with the remote control and see you laugh because you think it is cute unless you intend to let him continue to play with it. Once he has played with the buttons and seen your amused reaction, of course he will want to play with it again. It's better to err on the strict side and gradually release limits when children become mature enough to handle the responsibility or when you decide you don't mind that the behavior continues.

The challenge lies in deciding what you want ahead of time. It is better not to say, "I want you to stay in the living room to play," when you don't mean to enforce that. If a few minutes later you decide it's okay for the children to bring their toys into the kitchen and not to stay in the living room after all, you have taught them not to pay attention to the limits you set. It will help for you to think about what you say in the first place.

It is much harder to give too much freedom and then rein it in once a child has been given access to something. Resetting boundaries requires even more energy than holding to them firmly in the beginning. Be willing to demonstrate, practice, and follow through with what you would like for the children to learn.

> Often we expect children to read our minds and know how to do things they have never been taught. Take time to show needed steps for age-appropriate success.

For example, during cold weather, children can, with your support, place shoes in a basket, put mittens in a box, and hang a coat on a large hook. However, the shoes, mittens, and coats may end up on the floor. Remain consistent. Rather than simply picking up after the child sometimes, commenting other times, or leaving the items on the floor, teach the child and remind him of your expectations. Notice and comment positively when he puts his things away. Remember that the focus is to follow through on the routines that you decide are important.

You can gain insight about your children's behavior by watching what happens and then asking, "What does the child learn?"

- If Dad occasionally places his own coat over the back of a chair and drops his mittens on the table, the child learns that sometimes it's okay to put things away, and other times it's okay to leave them out.

- When Mom says, "I am tripping all over this stuff," as she steps over the boots and mittens but walks away, the child learns that words are just complaints and don't mean coats should be picked up.

- If Dad gets upset and says, "I told you four times to pick up your coat," the child learns that the parent doesn't get upset until the fourth time, and it is not important to listen or respond the first three times. He learns that the reason to be responsible with one's things is to avoid having someone get upset—rather than because responsibility for belongings is a valued trait.

Take time to talk with everyone involved with your child about which limits are important and which you want to let go. Success requires modeling, teaching, and following through with lots of support and encouragement.

Maintaining Consistency

Some of my friends do not decorate the Christmas tree on the bottom. I decided that I could teach my children what to do. I told them, "The tree is for looking—not for touching." They just love it. They look at it, but they don't touch. I followed through a couple times saying, "The tree is for looking—not for touching." I gave them a basket of beautiful but safe holiday items they could touch. One of my friends shared her experience. "I let my children use one finger to touch an ornament on the tree." But it didn't work for her. One finger led to whole hands touching. You have to start with "We look with our eyes, not touch with our hands." You have to set clear limits.

The structures you set keep order and security in your child's world. Define the limits, but within these boundaries children can be free in every way to explore, to express themselves, and to learn. Don't set boundaries arbitrarily. Use needed rules to teach children important lessons about respecting and caring for themselves and others.

Once you set limits that make sense, hold them firmly with kindness. "I know you want to go in Daddy's desk. There are lots of interesting things in there. You need to respect his things so he can do his work. However, playing office is a great idea. Would you like to play office on the kitchen table?" The goal is to help children get their needs met in constructive ways. They learn to be creative in problem solving and to honor the needs of others.

Sometimes, you may mean well but your timing is off. For example, you may say, "It's time to get out of the pool," or "It's time to go to bed." But if you don't follow through right then to get the child out of the pool or take your child to bed, it is better to wait until you have the energy and determination to follow through.

> Be firm but kind! When an expectation is set, be sure to reinforce it. Trust your intuition. If it doesn't feel right, don't let the child do it. Follow through and help your child complete a needed task or engage in a more positive way to get what is needed.

Inconsistency sends unintended or mixed messages and leads to a cycle of no fun. If you are inconsistent, your child doesn't do what you want because sometimes you want it and other times you don't. You become the nag-monster, and no one is happy. Your child learns that following the rules is not enjoyable and that participating in responsibility can bring frustration.

It is humbling to realize that, when it comes to children's behavior, the person who is in need of training is the parent! Children will do what they see us do and what they are used to doing with us. This means you have to make some decisions about your own behaviors if you want your children to do as you do. As you make limits fun and positive, children learn to be cooperative and to enjoy participating in family life. Following are four steps for success.

- **Be an example.** If you want your child to put away his boots, start by putting away your own. If you need to make some changes, say, "I have not done a good job about keeping things neat. I have been tripping on my boots. Here is where I am going to put them from now on."

- **Teach.** "I would like your boots to be put away, too. Here is where they go. Can you show me how you will put yours next to mine? When we put them away, they will be ready the next time we want to wear them."

- **Rehearse.** "Oops. I kicked off my boots under the table. What did I forget to do? Yes, thank you for reminding me where they go." Then practice putting them away together.

- **Give specific feedback and follow through.** Next time you come inside with your child, say, "I am proud of the way you are a good helper. When we go in, we can take off our boots together and put them away."

Soon you will find the routine becomes part of everyday behavior. If needed, you can revisit these steps.

Dinnertime together is one of the most important daily investments. Children who eat together with their parents bond as a family, have closer relationships, and develop conversation skills and manners. When mealtime needs a make-over, you can use the same steps: "We want to have more fun at meals, so we are going to (put away our phones, put down the books, set the table ahead of time, eat meals together, eat by candlelight)."

Say, "Tonight we are going to practice (putting our napkins on our laps, chewing with our mouths closed, sitting while we eat)." During the meal ask, "Is this where the napkin goes?" Place the napkin on your head. "Is this how we eat?" Chomp your food. After the laughter and feedback, be ready to thank everyone for working together. Then shift the conversation forward to your after-dinner walk to the park, or ask the children about their day. Mealtimes can become one of the most pleasurable time of your day.

You make the decisions about what you want your children to do. Your way may not be the same as your neighbor's way. However, once you decide on a plan, you can minimize behavior issues by following through. Children only know what you allow them to do, and they know if you will be firm. Being consistent is a gift that will keep on giving and will allow you to enjoy time together as a family.

Keeping Development in Mind

I had just yelled at the girls in the back seat to cut it out, when we passed a sign on a hospital billboard that said, "We treat the human spirit." I knew I wasn't being fair.

How do you know if your expectations are appropriate for your children? Perhaps you underestimate their capabilities and need to increase your expectations. On the other hand, you may expect too much and need to adjust. Keeping in mind what children are able to do at each age can help you become more aware of the support they need. For example, infants are engaged in nonstop exploration. Whatever is within reach is an invitation to touch and taste. Emotions are immediate. A crawler needs to be steered back to you. He giggles when you sneeze and laughs when the bottle drops. He thinks it is hilarious when you make funny faces and play peek-a-boo. With infants, you need to provide the following:

- Consistent security and reassurance

- Toys and objects that can be put in the mouth

- Verbal descriptions of objects and actions

- Appropriate stimulation and calming

- Attention at all times to ensure safety and comfort

Toddlers stay on the go. Their agenda includes climbing on the couch, taking apart a puzzle, figuring out how the trash container opens and closes, and confiscating the flashlight from the junk drawer that is left open. They would rather sit in the gift box than play with the gift and will crawl under the table rather than play with toys on top. Everything in sight still goes in their mouths with no discretion: paper clips, coins, bits of paper, and bottle tops. They are over, under, inside, and upside down as fast as they can go, always imitating the actions of others. This high-gear explosion of new learning will require a lot from you:

- Endless patience and boundless energy to keep up with ever-changing explorations

- Nonstop attention to safety

- Assistance with problem solving and arranging of toys and household items for imitative play

- Introducing words, answering questions, and redirecting to safe activities

Preschoolers love make-believe and use their vivid imagination to create dramatic stories of rescue and adventure. They talk to themselves while playing alone. Their need for stimulation seems constant. They dress up, create forts, stack pillows, balance block towers, and build with a variety of materials. They want Mom and Dad to do things with them. They like to go on errands, help get jobs done, and make a mess. Parents need to provide:

- Creativity and supplies to keep up with interests and ideas

- Discussions about how things work, with a review of steps and strategies

- Materials and opportunities for safe active play

- Monitoring to be sure children are not over- or understimulated

- Time and space for quiet time as well as active experiences

- Organization and support for growing competence in responsibility for belongings

The period beginning around age five is the golden time of childhood during which children attach to positive role models and love to have adults interested in what they do. They ask the bigger questions about life and have a natural thirst to know more about everything. They begin to think about other perspectives and develop a deeper sense of justice. Personal preferences and interests are easy to see, as they work intently on art or construction projects or show intensive focus on reading, dance, or sports. Children may idolize their heroes and role models. Parents need to:

- Meet the need for attention and extended time together

- Understand that development can be inconsistent

- Provide hands-on, active experiences

- Respect unique interests, strengths, and aptitudes

- Monitor exposure to media

- Remain vigilant for safety during risk-taking activities

- Support growing independence in choices and decisions

In addition to age-appropriate expectations, observe your child's behavior to determine whether or not he is in a frame of mind to contribute to activities. When children are tired or not feeling well, it is not a good time to start something that requires concentration. If your child has been sitting all morning, it may not be the best time to start a new project. If he needs a change of pace, redirect him to active play. Staying sensitive to your child's needs will give you the information to decide what is best.

> Is what you are expecting developmentally appropriate? Is your child capable of mastering what you ask, or will he become frustrated or discouraged?

When you are shopping, look for signs that your child is tired, and stop early, if possible, and head home. Even though you may prefer to have lunch out or visit a friend, think about whether or not this is a good choice for your child right now. Understanding if a child is tired or too young to sit still can help you be responsive.

Adjust your expectations when you see that your child is capable of zipping his coat, saying *please* and *thank you*, or helping clean his bedroom. However, you may also need to adjust your expectations when you see that sitting still for long periods of time brings frustration or digging out a messy room cannot be accomplished alone. Be sure that your child can do what you ask, and make sure that what you ask is fair.

Benefitting from Developmental Milestones

The Centers for Disease Control and Prevention provide comprehensive descriptions of the sequence of developmental milestones, organized by age. These allow you to follow age-appropriate expectations, and they provide common language to discuss development questions with your pediatrician. You can find this information at http://www.cdc.gov/ncbddd/actearly/milestones.

The American Academy of Pediatrics also provides information on developmental milestones, including information on toilet training and other practical issues, at http://www.healthychildren.org/English/ages-stages/prenatal/default.aspx. These resources provide a comprehensive overview and sequence for children's growth.

Planning Ahead

We had a trip prepared to visit my parents in Florida. Our three-year-old was excited to go. We got a book to read and practiced "flying" when we were riding in the car. On the day of the trip, we let him bring a little bag of his favorite cars, and we brought along the book about flying. Much to our relief, he handled it really well.

Children can be extremely reasonable about going along and cooperating if they know what to expect. If you have an infant and need to run errands, think about what supplies to take and how to schedule the sequence. Consider whether you have enough energy and determination to make it work. If you have a toddler, think about whether he can last that long or if he will be too tired to handle things. Preschool children need to know how to cope with feelings of disappointment, frustration, or tiredness. They may need support to engage themselves during a necessary wait. With older children, help them decide on age-appropriate ways to help you or to entertain themselves when you take them along.

Children without something constructive to do will satisfy their natural curiosity with creativity of their own. Their choices may be self-sustaining—daydreaming, watching others, or looking at a book—or they may seek entertainment with a game of Thumb War, giggling with a sibling, or another activity that you find distracting. A great strategy for all ages is to pack an emergency bag. If you end up staying out much longer than you planned, this will save the day. Consider including the following, and add anything else you think your children will need:

- Container with a snack and water

- Several favorite books

- Plastic bag filled with crayons, pencils, and a drawing or sticker book

- Pouch with special toys or small dolls

- Case or bag with quiet games, such as cards, a magnetic board, or word games

- Bag with a small pillow and comfort blanket

- Favorite stuffed animal or puppet

With preschool and school-age children, it helps to brainstorm about and practice the good manners they will need when they are guests in other people's homes. They will have fun practicing ahead of time, and your host will appreciate it. For example:

- Say, "Hello" and "Thank you for letting me come over."

- Eat food only when it is offered to you. Eat what is offered, and do not ask for something different. (Obviously, if your child has a food allergy, make the host aware of this ahead of time and consider sending your own snacks.)

- Ask permission if you are not sure you should do something.

- Use an indoor voice, and walk when inside the house.

- Put toys away before you leave.

- Say, "Thank you for the nice time."

Talking softly and whispering require practice. You may be surprised when you ask your young child to whisper to find he doesn't know how. You can whisper, "Night night," into his ear, and let him whisper it back to you. Or try, "Shhh. Let's whisper. Daddy is sleeping!" When you whisper together for fun, children will be better able to use a whisper or quiet voice when they are visiting.

> Let your child know ahead of time what to expect: "We can go outside and play for twenty minutes. Then, we have to come back in and get ready to leave." "We can play quiet games at Grandpa's house. Let's pack some to bring along."

Many wonderful books are available to help children prepare for family trips, school, or visits to the doctor or dentist. Find some at your local library and share them with your child. A few simple steps will make all the difference. An errand to the grocery store will be a positive experience after naptime when a child has rested and eaten. If he needs to stay in the cart, or if you have other plans for your time together, talk with him before you go to help him understand and agree to your expectations.

When you prepare your child, you also are preparing yourself. The forward focus can help you be intentional about the level of support needed for your child's success. Rehearse skills ahead of time to keep problems away and make your day go well.

Organizing a System that Works

As someone who gets joy in crossing things off my list, motherhood has made my world topsy-turvy. Some days it feels like nothing gets done. I heard about the survey of 7,000 mothers who said they suffer from Pinterest stress. I can relate. I feel inadequate, not because I need to be perfect, but because I just want to get organized.

Just like most adults, children need a system that works to keep things organized. The purpose of external order is to help children manage routines and activities with minimal frustration. Being able to find needed items reduces stress. The trick is to know each child well and to choose a system that works for your family. As soon as there is a meltdown or a missing item, it is time to revisit the plan.

Toddlers do well with toys in baskets that they can take off of shelves. Preschoolers often need help keeping things straight. It is much better to put some items away and pull them out for special reasons than to have so much available that the child cannot manage it independently. The number of toys available should be equal to what can be put away with minimal assistance.

School-age children can organize drawers with a system that they can keep up. They should be able to put away clothes and retrieve items easily. Some children may prefer hooks or hangers to drawers or shelves. The goal is independence, so that children have the ability to maintain order and find things as needed. This sense of mastery boosts confidence and minimizes problems.

Many issues can be solved with routines and organizational supports that work to keep belongings and activities on track. Here are additional suggestions to get organized:

- Use open stacking bins in a closet for underwear and socks instead of keeping them in drawers.

- Use a brightly colored minibucket in the bathroom or next to the bed to hold combs and hair products.

- For homework, set out a crate or basket with attached pouch for pencils, pens, scissors, and tape.

- Rely on a checklist for after-school or morning responsibilities.

- Keep backpacks, lunch boxes, and sports clothing ready to go in a basket or closet by the door.

- List or use pictures of steps or items needed to get ready for an activity.

- Get creative with organizers, such as a tackle box to sort small items or toys.

- Use a calendar with stickers to highlight activities and events.

There are many fun ways to include children in taking care of things, such as placing a squeegee in the shower that they can use to clean the glass after showering. Provide baskets or bins for bath toys. Remember to keep the expectations reasonable. Don't leave out the bubble-bath bottle or Mommy's make-up bag, which might be tempting to curious hands and minds.

> Thank the child before he does the task. This gentle reminder focuses attention on success. "Thank you for dropping your paper scraps into the can." "Thank you for putting your pajamas into the hamper."

Build responsibility, yet recognize that children are still developing the ability to refrain from touching what is not theirs. In an older child's room, keep items that are tempting to younger siblings up high. "Out of sight, out of mind" is a fair way to keep temptation away when curious young hands find an older sister's things interesting.

Give your children the gift of getting organized. Help them gain confidence and skills to take care of themselves. As they become more independent, they will develop pride in caring for their space. Start small and support them in making good choices about how to make things work. They will be glad to pitch in when they have a system to make it happen successfully.

Giving and Getting Attention

When my five-year-old, Emmett, is heading for bed, I ask, "What three jobs are on your checklist?" There isn't really a checklist. I just have him practice the three steps he needs to accomplish before I come in to read to him. I tell him to say the steps in his head before he does them. Of course, we said them out loud with him at first, but now that he is almost six, he can complete this routine independently. He has to get his pajamas on, brush his teeth, and choose three books. Once he is in bed, he calls, "Ready, Dad." I come for the reading and cuddling. It's a natural reward for his success.

Some of us find that we rise to the occasion when handling moments of crisis. Yet, the little frustrations can cause us to become unglued or distracted. Instead of waiting for irritations to happen and then trying to fix them, support your children—and yourself—by thinking about how you get and give attention.

Set your children up for success by minimizing the triggers to their frustration. It isn't that you want to remove challenges or make life easy but that you do want to decrease unnecessary stress. You need a way to get your children's attention, help them remember what needs to be done, and get them to ask for what they need. The following can help as you think about how to make your communication more successful.

- **Get their attention.** A child engaged in play won't always hear a call from across the house. Unless there is an emergency, go to your child and make eye contact before you communicate. When you are near, you can pat his shoulder or lay your hand on his arm, to connect. If your child is playing outside, ring a bell or call out a special word you have chosen that means "right away." When you take the time to go to your children when you need them, they will learn the practice of coming to get you rather than yell for you from another room.

- **Get your attention.** A pinky squeeze is a great way for a child to tell you that he wants something, without interrupting. To show your child that you will be finished shortly, you can pinky-squeeze back and then give your attention as soon as you are free.

- **Use sign language.** There are many websites that show the American Sign Language signs for *more, all done, drink, bathroom,* and other important words. Using signs can help younger children communicate their wants and needs.

- **Make one-on-one time.** Sometimes a child just needs and wants to talk. Find a place where you can go off together and connect. You can ask what happened or find out what your child thinks can be done to solve a problem. Private bonding sets a pattern of trust and communication that will continue through the teen years.

- **Fill the emotional tank**. Sometimes, your children just need you to stop what you are doing and spend a few minutes with them. When your child comes to hug you, put aside what you are doing and return the hug. In these moments, he may share something profound, sweet, or funny.

- **Take time to play.** Research by Grazyna Kochanska et al. and by Sharon Ray shows that when parents spend positive playtime with their children, it boosts cooperation, willingness to help, and responsiveness. Shake those rattles, play peekaboo, build with blocks, paint together, or play card and board games. Outdoor play, hide-and-seek, jump rope, and ball games teach turn-taking and cooperation. Play time will spill over into happy teamwork when work needs to be done.

- **Rehearse needed steps.** Talking through plans allows you to find out what your child knows. "What are we doing before bed?" "What do we need to do before we get in the car?" When you ask, you will find out what your child does and doesn't understand. Talking together helps children feel included.

> Children want and need individual time with the undivided focus that makes them feel special. Put distractions away, make eye contact, and take time to listen. Spend at least fifteen uninterrupted minutes with each child every day.

Be sure each child has enough of you. Spend private time every day so that your child can count on your undivided focus. Let him lead the conversation and activity. Make sure to plan Mom or Dad dates with a special walk, breakfast out, or another activity. Keep in mind what it feels like to be a child and to be dependent on someone else for everything, including affirmation. Telling your children you love them is very powerful.

Managing Technology Use

I volunteer for after-school pickup at my daughter's pre-K, and I see parents pull up in their cars, talking on the phone while children buckle themselves in. I want to look my daughter in the eye and ask her about her day. I only see her in the morning and after school. I want to be her favorite time of day.

Technology can make parenting and life easier. Information is at your fingertips with Facebook, advice blogs, food reviews, and twenty-four–hour news. GPS gets you where you need to go. Toy-of-the-month clubs deliver craft and construction kits to the front door. Your car even may have automated scanning for hands-free parking. If you have a question, there's an app for that. Many people love the immediate gratification and thrive on instant access to the ones they care about.

There is a humorous side, too, such as texting your spouse to come downstairs or sending a photo from the grocery store to clarify a needed brand. Over morning coffee when you haven't slept, it can be a relief to check the funny videos and read bleary-eyed parent posts on social media. The laughter can make you feel less isolated when you're facing the dishes, the dog, and children who need to get to school.

The challenge with technology is keeping it in perspective. It is a tool that can make parenting easier, but don't let it interfere with your being an attentive, focused parent. The phone won't help you as you tuck your children in. At the park, when your child calls, "Look at me!" lay the phone aside for a moment and be present. Your children need your attention and will look for it any way they can get it. Digital connections are important, but the one who needs your connection most is the child in front of you.

It will take effort and determination to set limits. If your family's technology habits need changing, try cutting back gradually. If going cold turkey works better, anticipate that putting away the phone can make you feel anxious. One mom said, "We put a basket by the front door, and during family time, every phone goes in that basket. It changed everything. My relationship with my husband improved drastically, and we started having fun with our children again."

> Make sure you have taken care of your personal business (checking your social networking site, e-mail, texting) so that you can give your full and undivided attention to your child.

The goal is to focus on the connections with your children in a new and purposeful way. Here are some suggestions to get started:

- **Be consistent.** Have phone-free times that are nonnegotiable.
- **Leave the house.** Visit a relative or attend a community child-friendly event, without taking your phone along.

- **Eat dinner together.** Put the phones away, and try candlelight, new foods, or themes that make conversation fun.

- **Put your child in charge.** Take your child shopping for a menu he has chosen, and make a meal together.

- **Create family fun.** Have game nights. Hold a dance party and enjoy music together with a costume theme. Institute a movie night. Focus on animals, travel, or other topics that you can talk about together.

- **Get into nature.** Explore the outdoors. Nature is the best teaching tool. If you can't go out, bring collections inside, such as pinecones, twigs, and leaves to view with a magnifier.

Don't let screen time take over snuggle time. When you do watch TV, aim for times when the children are asleep. Monitor news stories and make sure children are not exposed to frightening images, especially those that play over and over. Mindful review and thoughtful planning can make a big difference. The habits and patterns you set now will continue through the teen years.

The American Academy of Pediatrics states that children under the age of two should have no exposure to media, and children older than two should have a one- to two-hour limit with supervision through age twelve. Researchers Dimitri Christakis et al., Angeline Lillard and Jennifer Peterson, Jennifer Manganello and Catherine Taylor, and Frederick Zimmerman et al., among others, have found that for every hour of TV children watch, their odds of attention problems, decreased language skills, behavior problems, and bullying increase significantly. Media use requires ongoing, diligent parental guidance. Without careful monitoring, media use can become a detrimental influence.

Handling Pester Power

I know I should say no more often. But truthfully, fun for my son means fun for me. I get to help him put things together. It's like a quick fix for boredom, and he knows I like doing it with him. It's a habit and problem, but I don't know how to stop giving in. When I say no, it brings on a scene. It's my own fault because I am the one who keeps buying him stuff.

Dealing with pester power is one of the greatest challenges of parenthood. "Daddy, please, please can I have it? I was good on the way here. I want one so bad." When a new movie is released, the characters are already in the grocery store, on cereal boxes, in songs, and in the toy market. The message "Buy me now!" is everywhere.

According to the Public Health Advocacy Institute at the Northeastern University School of Law, nag power directly influences more than $330 billion in sales each year for children ages four to twelve. Researchers Mary Story and Simone French found that when children beg, parents give in with soda, cookies, and candy up to 60 percent of the time. The reasons most parents gave in was because an item was inexpensive or the item was used as a reward for good behavior. Whether with sugar cereal, snacks, or toys, pestering is a challenge that most parents dread. Without purposeful planning, pestering can be a habit that is hard to change.

How can you counteract the pressure and set limits? The following tips can help you prepare and handle things with confidence.

- **Remember that out of sight is out of mind.** Protect toddlers and young children from advertising and from exposure to treats, such as the candy aisle at the grocery store. When you need to purchase items from a toy store, do so when your children are not present.

- **Tell children ahead of time what to expect.** "We are going grocery shopping. You may choose one fruit for yourself and help me load food on the checkout counter. We will be buying only what is on our list today." "We are going to get a present for James but not for ourselves. We can talk about things we like, but today, we are only going to buy the present for the party."

- **Use cash.** Letting children hold ten or twenty dollars in cash can show them that there is a limit to what you will spend today. When children see a credit card, they do not understand the connection between the plastic and limits on spending.

- **Counteract entitlement.** Let children earn items that are not for birthdays or holidays. When your child wants a toy, let him help you with a project or chore. Seeing dollar bills add up one by one in a jar over time can instill the important connection between effort and money. In addition, this teaches children the important skill of waiting.

- **Educate children about the facts.** Explain that food companies use characters and advertising to make children want their products. Talk about unsafe ingredients and the need for healthy foods.

- **Give thanks.** Share genuine thankfulness for what you have. Rather than talk about the kitchen or bathroom you dream about or the clothing you wish you had, let your children overhear you being thankful for the good things in your life.

> Instead of yelling or raising your voice, surprise your children by lowering your voice to a whisper. It helps you to stay in control and think more clearly, and it draws children's attention.

Delayed gratification is a needed strength. If you give in to every whim in childhood, how will your children learn to say no or wait when they are teens? This greater goal can help you stay firm when your children are younger.

When your children do pester you and you feel at wits' end, keep your cool. The sooner children realize you are going to hold the line, the more quickly they will turn their attention to other things. Say, "I am sorry. I know you want it. We are not going to get it today for any reason." Then turn your attention to what is ahead. "Let's hurry home and get lunch." When you feel like raising your voice, turn down the volume, keep calm, and carry on.

Building Competence

When my fourth child needed multiple heart surgeries, I felt so bad for him that I gave in to everything. He'd want pancakes, and I'd say okay. Then he wanted chicken nuggets, and I would fall all over myself to get them. My husband finally stepped in and said, "You need to eat what your mom makes you." I realized that because I felt guilty I had let all the structure go. My emotions got in the way. I needed to get objective and see that my son needed consistency and limits, just like my other kids.

When things go wrong, instead of flipping out or melting down, think about how to use daily events to teach. It is normal for children to have preferences and to be impulsive. Knowing they are still learning to think before they act can help you be more patient and realize that mistakes are opportunities to learn. There are some important ideas to get across to your children:

- **Sometimes you have to wait, can't have what you want, and need to be patient.** Limits are an important part of life. There will be times when your children are disappointed. At those moments, you can show kindness, validation, and support. Your children will be happier and will feel secure when they know you are looking out for their best interest.

- **It's okay to make mistakes.** We can learn from our choices. "I forgot to bring in my rain boots, so water got inside. I need to put them over the heat vent until they dry. Next time, I will remember to bring them in." No one is perfect, and your children learn from the way you handle your own mistakes. The next time your child takes off his boots outside, you can say, "Remember what happened when I did that?"

> Teach children the correct procedures and behaviors. It is much harder to go back and undo a learned behavior. Children need to see, understand, and be able to carry out expectations.

- **Strategies matter.** Tweaking your strategies pays off. "My hands were wet, and the plate slipped out and broke. Next time, I will dry my hands before I pick up a plate." Children learn that even when you feel upset, you can talk through what happened and plan a better approach for next time.

- **Actions have consequences.** Make connections between decisions now and consequences later. For example, your children may want to drop their bikes on the lawn or leave the basketball outside before coming in for dinner. Remind them, "Keeping bikes dry makes them last a long time and not get rusty." "Putting the ball away in the basket will help you find it later." Once they know, a simple reminder can help: "Bikes away." "Balls go in the basket."

- **Thinking works.** Teaching children to think, rather than getting upset with them, helps them develop understanding and take responsibility for their actions. Ask, "What can we do to make this work?" "What else can we do?" Help your children develop the ability to think before they act.

Unforeseen issues may happen. But every day, you make progress in the direction of your goals. Choosing expectations wisely, planning ahead, and understanding the level of support children need can help things go much more smoothly.

CHAPTER 4
USING EFFECTIVE POSITIVE GUIDANCE

Defining Positive Guidance

We are so busy just getting through the day that we often don't think about what our daughter will be later in life. Her teacher told us she is a leader. She loves to help at home and she has great ideas, but I get irritated and yell at her when she has to have things her own way. I want her to feel great about who she is and use her strengths in positive ways.

If you don't remember what happened to you when you were young, you will quickly find out when you become a parent. Words that you once heard will come flying out of your mouth in a moment of frustration: "You are grounded." "Do it because I say so." "What's wrong with you?" "Obey me right now." These deeply ingrained messages can pop out before you stop them or consider their impact.

When things go wrong, it is easy to get upset or yell, especially when you feel stressed and at your limit. Even the best of us may respond punitively if we lack effective strategies to redirect and guide children in positive ways. You may wish you could take back, rewind, or edit what you have said, realizing that you made matters worse. By understanding the difference between discipline and punishment, you can interrupt the negative patterns and create what you really want for your children and yourself.

Often when people say, "That child needs a little discipline," what they really mean is that they think the child needs to be punished. But punishment causes more problems than it solves. Punishment focuses on what a child cannot do. It is based on the belief that pain, shame, or embarrassment will motivate behavior change. In fact, researchers Rosemary Mills et al. and Elizabeth Gershoff assert that punishment does the opposite. Resulting shame causes a child to disconnect. The stress she feels from adult anger or inflicted pain actually makes her less able to focus and less likely to remember a needed lesson or skill. Punishment makes a child dependent on someone else to intervene rather than instilling the understanding, skill, and self-regulation needed to ensure success. Both the child and parent remain frustrated.

Using shame or pain denies a child's human need for nurture, safety, kindness, and respect. It disconnects a child from sensitivity to her body, mind, and spirit. These are the very things we want to build up—the awareness of the body and what it does, the ability to think before acting, and an open conscience with empathy to the needs of self and others.

Punishment relies on the parent's anger, power, and coercion. Not only does this break the needed emotional connection of trust, but it models a message about the use of power that is the opposite of what we hope to convey. The child learns to use his own power over others instead of responding with sensitivity and solving problems by talking them out.

Punishment plants seeds of self-doubt rather than self-confidence. The child grows up to struggle with feelings of lowered self-worth from being hit, hurt, or shamed. Research shows that repeated use of spanking is detrimental to self-esteem and lowers mental health. According to researchers Elizabeth Gershoff and Andrew Grogan-Taylor, we often see this in self-defeating and addictive behaviors rather than in self-respect and healthy choices during the teen and adult years. A threat may seem to stop a behavior, but the child only stops temporarily out of fear. The same pattern of behavior occurs again—often over and over. Children comply without learning to be thoughtful about the needs of self or others. Punishment makes the child feel like a failure—incapable of making positive choices without the threat or coercion from others.

Physical punishment, such as hitting, slapping, and spanking, consistently has been shown by Gershoff's review of the research to be detrimental to children's life-long mental health, with no evidence that it yields benefits or that it influences positive behavior. Punitive approaches lead to shame-based self-evaluation: "I am bad." As asserted by Louis Cozolino, author of *The Neuroscience of Human Relationships,* and Darcia Narvaez in her chapter in *Children's Moral Emotions and Moral Cognition,* and reaffirmed by UNICEF in the publication *Building Better Brains: New Frontiers in Early Childhood Development,* through neuroscience research, we are able to understand that every child needs security, safety, and positive approaches to guidance, which lead to self-regulation, empathy, compassion, and to ongoing spiritual and psychological wholeness.

In contrast, positive guidance focuses on teaching children the skills they need to be successful. *Guidance* means to give counsel, direction and instruction. Guidance empowers children with understanding. With guidance, children make a memory of success so that they learn what to do next time. This approach reorients the role of the parent as a positive model to support and build competence.

Rather than making children do something, "because I said so," the goal is to instill authentic cooperation. Help children learn to do the good thing because they want to and because they have come to love doing kind things for others. When supported and respected, children will become caring because they truly are empathetic and sensitive to others. Help them to find a sense of purpose and identity as a compassionate and responsible human being—and to know that their actions and words matter. These strengths do not come from coercion but instead from loving relationships and caring guidance.

Come alongside your children to support success, and foster inner regulation and sensitivity to others. Children stay connected because they know you have their best interest at heart. Protect their deep need for empathy and respect, so that they remain open to your guidance.

When things don't go well, instead of disconnecting or getting angry, you can learn to do the opposite. When your child is a wreck and you are beside yourself, you can turn

> Always remember that you are the grown up and are ultimately responsible for the way things turn out. Your child does not have your judgment or history of experiences and can't be held responsible for the ultimate outcome.

things around by connecting with sensitivity and care. Use each opportunity to help yourself and your child learn to handle situations better.

Positive relational guidance helps you respond to behavior effectively and avoid common frustrations. If you tire of being the behavior police or want to unravel power struggles, you can learn what works to boost cooperation. You can strengthen your relationships as you build children's competence and make your time with them a pleasure.

Practicing a Positive Perspective

As a father, I can see the power of being positive. To choose life in the gratitude zone and realize that the children will go there with you is life changing. I teach the boys that they are masters of their own "attitude destiny." They like being masters of anything!

The most influential person in your child's life is you! Perhaps someone has commented, "Your son mixes his cereal around in the milk just like you do." Or, "I love how your daughter laughs just like you. She has your sense of humor." You can be sure that your children are following in your footsteps.

The greatest lessons you will ever teach are the ones you model. How do you respond when something goes wrong? Do you find ways to make fun out of challenges? How do you handle things when others are upset? What do you say when you are under stress? Most importantly, do you take the time to really listen when your children need you? When your child has done something wrong or has made a mistake, what kind of response do you have? In these everyday interactions, you can show patience, generosity, flexibility, humor, kindness, and respect.

We all know a parent who leans over the seat of the car and yells, "Be quiet back there!" It's easy to see the irony if a person uses the same behavior that he just asked his child to stop using. In your home, do you come right away when your spouse or partner says, "It's time to leave," or do you keep messaging on your phone or working on the computer? If you keep on working at the computer, how can you be surprised when your child does not come right away when you call her?

Ever struggle with feeding healthy food to a child, all the while knowing your secret stash of candy bars that's hidden in the cupboard? It makes good sense to model the behaviors you want your children to have. On a practical level, positive behavior starts with you.

Children have an uncanny way of taking on the subtle traits we wish maybe they wouldn't. Sometimes, these issues are minor and might make you laugh. Other times, it helps to be more understanding when you realize where the child learned the behavior: "My son leaves everything for the last minute. I know he got that from me." The idea is not to blame but simply to understand that children are naturally going to pick up and repeat the behaviors that they see around them.

> Model the behavior you want. Children are watching all the time, and they will grow up to be like you—whether you want them to or not. They will learn from your example.

It helps to think about the behaviors you want your children to have. The following is a good checklist to help you be aware of what they observe in the way you handle your emotions.

- When I have expectations and feel let down, how do I respond?

- When things have gone wrong, do I focus right away on creating a new path to success?

- When I don't feel well, do I respond thoughtfully to my needs in healthy ways?

- When I feel stressed, do I take steps to calm myself and reorient my emotional direction?

- Do I ask for help or explain what I need before I get out of sorts or discouraged?

- Do I show kindness and caring when someone is in my way or holding up my plans?

The incredible secret of effective parenting begins with your own modeling. If you want your children to develop patience, empathy, and thoughtfulness, they must see you exhibiting these traits in your actions. This awareness can jumpstart meaningful change in yourself as well as in your relationships with others. It can inspire you to be honest and authentic in the way you seek to grow.

Identifying Behavior Success Stoppers

When my five-year-old son had a babysitter, they had to pick up something from her dentist. On the way, they stopped at a grocery store and stood in front of the bakery case. José said, "We don't eat that. It's all sugar." In the moment, he could have said, "I'll have one," but all the stuff we told him about sweets made him adamant. He came home to tell me about it. I was so excited to see that he was listening.

Think about how challenging it is to change your own habits. Yet we sometimes expect children to be able to change their behavior instantly. If you use tricks or techniques in parenting and they don't work, it is easy to come to the conclusion that you have failed or that your child cannot or will not change. Continuing responses and behaviors that do not help—yet expecting different results—can keep you from exploring new approaches.

When behavior needs support or it is time for a new approach, it can help to uncover some hidden success stoppers. Once you clearly see what you are doing and understand why it is not working, you can replace this approach with effective strategies. You will keep your relationship with your children, and your confidence in them, strong.

Many people use threats to get what they want from a child: "Either play nicely or take a time out." "Either stop that or you won't get to watch the movie." "Walk next to me or we are going home." The problem here is that this approach means threatening to remove something that is actually in the child's best interest—you want him to play with his friend or see the movie. You want to enjoy your walk together.

Power struggles cause a child to work against, instead of with, you. Power struggles actually work against the goals they are intended to achieve. Demands are always a power struggle, because these give the child the power to refuse. "Come here right now." What will you do if he doesn't? Threats give a statement of intention to give punishment. The child is told she will get what she does not want, such as five minutes in the corner, or will have something taken away that she does want, such as time to play. "If you do not take your bike in, you will lose it for a week." "If you do not stop all that noise, your friend will have to go home." The child may choose to lose her bike for a week rather than bring it in, and you will have to deal with her boredom. The children playing loudly may be wound up and need help to refocus their energy. Sending the friend home will leave you to find another activity to do with your child.

The problem here is that you do want your child to play nicely, not to have a time out or have the friend sent home. You want her to ride her bike and get her energy out. At first threats may work, because the child fears losing what she wants. However, she is only complying through external control, not because she feels in charge of her own decisions. She hasn't learned to cooperate from her own will, her internal control. Making a child obey out of fear robs the child of the joy and pride of doing something cooperative. Internal regulation is the goal.

Over time, making threats causes a child to tune out. This is especially true if you are inconsistent in carrying out the consequences. If, for example, a parent says, "I have talked to you about running in the mall ten times. Stop doing that!" this shows that for the first nine times, the child wasn't listening and the parent wasn't following through. A more effective approach is to say, "I understand that you feel like running. When we get home and people are not around, you can run around to your heart's content." That response helps the child learn how to get her needs met in safe and healthy ways.

Power struggles hook you into an ineffective and discouraging cycle of frustration. Of course, you need to step in when a child is in danger or out of control and could hurt himself or others. But don't rely on power and coercion instead of instilling cooperation. Shift responsibility in age-appropriate ways to the child. By shifting ownership to the child, you build inner regulation and independence.

Positive guidance influences rather than controls behavior. It focuses children's attention on what needs to be done and motivates respectful ways of thinking and caring. Guidance instills essential habits of mind that result in self-directed behavior and empowers inner strengths, needed character traits, and a true willingness of spirit. As you shift away from power struggles, you will see your children in a new light. They will begin to grow in remarkable ways. They will become thoughtful and considerate and will be able to tune in to the moment and the needs of others around them. They will take pride in bringing joy and satisfaction to themselves and to others.

Replacing—Rather than Stopping—Misbehavior

I cleaned out the lower cupboard in the kitchen and filled it with plastic containers and other safe utensils. We put Charlie and Rose's play kitchen along the wall and painted a cardboard stovetop and attached it to a chair. Now my little chefs are busy cooking while I make dinner.

Many people think of behavior guidance as stopping misbehavior. Stopping a behavior merely ends it for the moment. Instead, shift your attention and learn to replace, rather than to stop, unwanted behaviors. Redirect the child to a healthy, fun, or helpful behavior, without drawing attention to the unwanted behavior. When you want to stop a behavior, you need to put another behavior in its place.

You may be asking, "If I don't point out the misbehavior directly, how does my child know not to do it?" The answer is that when you redirect behavior to another option, the child internalizes a lesson. The lesson is not that a behavior is bad, but that there are positive alternatives and healthier or safer ways to get her needs met. For example, if a younger child is climbing on the table, instead of saying, "Don't climb on the table. It isn't safe," help the child down. Then say, "Let's stay on the floor where it is safe." One is the negative—what not to do. The other is the positive alternative—what to do. This may sound minor, but the first approach involves giving attention to and stopping an ineffective or undesired behavior; whereas, the second approach involves focusing the child's attention on and training the habit of the new behavior.

The idea is to give a child something to do that is not compatible with the undesired behavior. Describe what you would like her to do instead. This way you get the child's mind off of what she was doing and shift her attention to the more productive or safer behavior. It may take practice to think about what you do want and to focus on the positive outcome you want to create. Here are some examples of what to say:

- **For Infants**

  - ▸ Keep your food on the tray. (Instead of "Don't throw the peas.")

  - ▸ Let's keep your socks on. (Instead of "Don't take off your socks.")

  - ▸ Let's go to the kitchen to watch Nana. (Instead of "Don't crawl into the bathroom.")

- **For Toddlers**

  - ▸ The paintbrush goes in the water. (Instead of "Don't put the brush in your mouth.")

  - ▸ The soap squirts into the bathtub with the toys. (Instead of "Don't squirt the soap on the floor.")

- ► Come help me roll the playdough. (Instead of "Stop touching the pencils.")

- ► Let's play hide-and-seek in the living room. (Instead of "Get out of the closet.")

- **For Preschool and School-Age Children**

    - ► We need to cover the table with a mat before we color. (Instead of "I told you not to use markers on the bare table.")

    - ► Come help me arrange the orange slices on the plate. (Instead of "Will you leave your sister alone?")

    - ► Let's go jump on the trampoline. (Instead of "Get off that couch right now!")

    - ► You may throw the ball in the basement. (Instead of "Stop throwing the ball in the living room.")

Redirecting energy with an incompatible alternative will become a huge help to you. Children can't jump on the beds, but they can go outside and jump on a trampoline or run around. They can't throw balls in the living room, but they can throw bean bags in the hall. One mother asked her five sons to run around the house ten times before dinner each day, even in the snowy winter, because she was determined that they would sit together as a family to eat. On long car trips, they all did jumping jacks together at the rest stops. Refocusing energy into positive activities will make a big difference, especially as children get older. Be creative and respectful in redirecting children toward positive solutions. Invite cooperation and teach them needed guidelines in positive ways.

> Give the child something to do that is incompatible with the unwanted behavior. Say, "Let's pretend we are on a secret mission and see if we can sneak upstairs without anyone hearing us." If a child is running around, instead of mentioning it, simply ask him to help you by putting the cereal boxes on the shelf.

Turning Children on to Cooperation

When I go out to the store and want to bring along something for my child to play with, we put small toys in a lunchbox, and he is responsible for bringing what he wants. My toddler loves this and plays happily in the car with what he has packed for himself.

Parents may think of cooperation as a child doing what you say to do, but this is not cooperation—it's compliance. Children are more likely to comply with requests when they are given appropriate control and mastery in their lives. *Cooperation* is willing engagement in a mutual goal. Children who can take ownership in their plans are highly motivated to cooperate in positive ways with needed tasks.

Of course there will be times, such as in a time crunch or when your child's safety is in question, when you need to gather up your child and hurry to the car or move quickly to another place. But generally, giving children a choice empowers them. It activates their inner cooperation and helps build their independence.

As children get older, they will face countless choices, some that are inconsequential and others that may be life changing or even dangerous. So, start when they are very young and gradually help them flex their choice muscles. Giving positive choices about how to accomplish something teaches children that there are many ways to create positive outcomes and that they always have a choice.

To do this effectively, first state what needs to be done. Then, offer two ways to go about it. For example, "We need to hold hands in the parking lot. Do you want to hold my left hand or my right hand?" "It's cold outside. We need to zip coats. Do you want to zip by yourself or do you need my help?" "Your homework is waiting. Do you want to do it now or right after dinner?"

> Give the child two choices, both of which are positive and acceptable to you. "Would you rather tiptoe or hop to the bathroom?" "It's time to get in the car. Do you want to wear your sneakers or your boots?" State what needs doing. Give two positive choices. Then say, "You choose or I'll choose."

By modeling specific choices, you show your children what kinds of options are available. It takes practice to think of two good ways to get something done.

If the child does not choose, restate the options only once, then say, "You choose or I'll choose." Then follow through—if the child still does not choose, choose for her. The next time she is in that situation, she will know that you will give two choices and will follow through. The power struggle has been removed. By taking this approach, you retain authority to assure the needed outcome, but you transfer the responsibility of ownership to the child. This step of transfer is essential to building true cooperation and willingness. "It's time to go up to bed. Do you want to go up with Daddy or Mommy?" Once the child starts up the stairs, it is because of her own choice. Ownership increases responsibility.

Active participation helps children feel more in control of what happens to them. They are more likely to cooperate because they can choose the response that works best for them. The current success increases future success, because children know and have practiced what works.

Sometimes children show a strong preference for clothing. For example, you and your family are going to your mother's house, and you have picked out clothes for your daughter to wear. "We are going to Grandma's. It's okay if you wear your blue dress or your purple pants and pink flowered shirt. Which do you prefer?" If your daughter replies, "I want to wear my red princess dress," you can say, "Blue dress or purple pants and pink shirt. You choose or I'll choose." Then, whisper in her ear that the red princess dress will be waiting for her when she comes home. If she hesitates, you choose one outfit while quickly making conversation about an activity Grandma has waiting. Move forward with confidence. Sometimes, a clothing choice is important, and sometimes it is not. Of course, if you don't mind, you can avoid the whole conversation by letting her wear the red dress in the first place.

Following are more ideas for offering choices:

- **During the morning routine:** We need to get dressed. Do you want to put on your shirt first or your pants first?

- **At bath time:** Do you want to swim like a turtle or wiggle like a fish to rinse off the soap?

- **During the bedtime routine:** It's time to brush your teeth. Would you like to do it in two minutes or three?

- **When it's time to leave the playground:** It's almost time to go home. Do you want to leave in five minutes or six minutes?

- **When your child needs a drink:** I see you are thirsty. Do you want to drink from the blue cup or the red cup?

- **To redirect to a safer activity:** We can play in the backyard. Do you want the hoops or the balls?

- **To engage the child in helping at the grocery store:** We need bagels. You may choose cinnamon or plain.

- **When it's time to clean up:** We need to clean up the paints. Do you want to carry the box or the brush?

- **At dinner time:** We need to set the table. Which side of the table do you want to wipe? I'll wipe the other side. We make a good cleaning team.

- **When you need to be quiet:** Do you want to tiptoe like a kitty or creep like a deer past the room where your sister is taking a nap?

Children have wonderful imaginations and soon will be helping create choices that are sweet and entertaining.

Many parents ask whether positive incentives are a good idea. These can be useful at times for preschool or school-aged children to activate a new behavior. However, as Alfie Kohn points out in his book *Punished by Rewards,* research shows that using incentives for behaviors that are already established can cause children to invest less effort to get something done, so these should be used with caution and sparingly.

An incentive works best when it functions as a cue or reminder related to a task. For example, give your child a task to complete each day when she comes home from school. Write the task on index cards (or use pictures if she can't read yet). Clip the cards to a piece of poster board or pin them on a bulletin board where she can see them. Then, when she completes the task, she can move one card from the "To Do" side of the board to the "Done" side. When she completes the responsibilities without a reminder for five days, she earns an agreed-upon activity. A school-aged child who gets to bed on time for five days might earn fifteen minutes of extra reading with Dad before lights out. Add the successes until the child reaches the goal, even if this is not accomplished five days in a row. An incentive will work only if it is something the child wants and the task is one the child can accomplish independently. If there is intrinsic value, such as earning a special lunch with Mom or earning a video night with Dad, it can be effective. Ultimately, the goal is to build cooperation for the sake of pride in accomplishment and joy of competence. Used sparingly—and when the child wants to try it—an incentive can be a fun way to jump-start a new habit.

According to researchers Mireille Joussemet, Renee Landry, and Richard Koestner, children are born with the drive to feel competent. They are active participants from birth—eagerly invested and motivated to contribute and care. They take pride in their growing ability to do things for themselves and love to contribute to the happiness of others. Foster success by giving lots of practice in making good choices. Children will join in eagerly because you have transferred the responsibility to them. They will see the result of their decisions, knowing they made good things happen and knowing how to create those results again.

The goal is not to punish your child but to help her learn. "When you have put your toys away, then you may come and have a snack." If the child doesn't put her toys away but comes to the table, then you have to take her by the hand and quietly walk her back to her toys. Don't let it go or act as if you didn't notice that he didn't do as you asked.

Children need to know that you have a bottom line. You have to mean what you say and follow through. Your child needs to see that you are firm in your expectations— and that you will do what you have said you will do. You have to be willing to abandon the shopping cart at the store, leave the game at the park, or walk out of an event, gather the children, and go home.

You can prepare your children ahead of time and encourage active participation. "When your closet is finished, then you may go to your friend's house. Do you want to talk over how you will get it done?" If the child agrees and understands that the closet must come first, then she cannot go to play at her friend's house until her responsibility is finished. When the closet is finished, then she may go. Perhaps she will only have one hour today to play, instead of two. Perhaps she will not be able to go to her friend's house today. Time at the friend's house is the result of a fulfilled responsibility, not a reward for success or punishment for failure.

When you expend the energy to help children become more responsible and make good choices, they will respect you and themselves. Encourage growing self-regulation and equip them to navigate the daily challenges and joys of their lives. This is a satisfying way to approach parenting, because you get to see the results as children become competent and caring.

Shifting the Focus Forward

The children were calling each other poo poo *and* doo-doo head. *They were giggling and making faces. I told them, "When I was young, we each chose a vegetable name to call each other for a whole day. Much to my surprise, Charlotte said, "I want to be Carrots." "I want to be Broccoli!" laughed her brother. Their friend Zooey said, "I am Beanie." In an instant, they switched directions in their thinking and ran off to the swing set. Without making a big deal, the children got the lesson that they could have fun without repeating something silly.*

Children often shout, "Look at me! Look at me!" Parents usually encourage them to take pride in their new skills, knowing that they love when we care and notice. You might clap your hands and cheer when your toddler kicks the ball back to you. You might thank your preschooler for being a good helper. As your child reaches school age, you might make a big deal when she accomplishes something new.

But when children throw food, knock something over, or jump on the couch, you might make a big deal over this behavior as well. When you draw attention to behavior and reinforce it by making a fuss, you turn the situation into a power struggle. Acting as the behavior police is exhausting and makes parenting no fun at all.

Similar to the positive approach to getting your child to cooperate, when your child engages in behavior that isn't dangerous, destructive, or embarrassing—but is unwanted nonetheless—invest your energy wisely. Ignore minor misbehavior. Pretend that you didn't hear, move away, or focus on something else. As long as your child is safe and happy, ignore wiggling, whining, or slobbering while he brushes teeth. Take your eyes away completely, as if it never happened. This action works extremely well to reduce issues. Rather than expending energy on stopping a behavior, focus on what you do want the child to do. For example, if your baby is learning to walk, quietly steer her away from the phone charger and say, "Let's play with the wagon." Move the dog dish out of reach, and replace it with a ball and cup your toddler can touch. Take the steam out of a situation when you say softly, "Hitting hurts. Let's be gentle," as you stroke your toddler's hand. When you are consistent, you reinforce the boundaries and expectations.

Toddlers discover new things by the minute. They have intense feelings. Everything is exciting as they learn they have the ability to make things happen. They are just discovering their limits, their energy, and their interests. They like to run, jump, and throw things. Rather than making a big deal of the unwanted behavior, minimize your emotional response.

Invest in building the skills you do want. For example, find ways to let your toddler help out. Show her how to feed the dog; ask for her help to scoop the food and pour it in the dish. Include your child in activities that make her feel excited about participating in family life. Show her how to make safe decisions that are fun, and help her get what she needs in satisfying ways.

When you make unwanted behaviors a nonissue, your child will move on. The wigging will pass. She will forget about slobbering while brushing her teeth. She will give up whining when there is no response from you. Give positive feedback when you see behaviors that you value: "You were so thoughtful to help your dad carry the books." "I appreciate so much that you set the table." "I love how you had fun in the bath with your sister." "You asked to borrow the pencil in such a polite tone of voice." Your children will know that you notice and care when they are being responsible and kind.

Train yourself to describe the respectful behaviors when you see them: "Great! Your boots are put away on the mat." "You are hanging up your coat with two hands." "Your backpack fits perfectly inside the rack." This narration and specific feedback helps children focus on the actions and strategies that work.

Ask children for input. "What work best for you? What can we do to make this better next time?" Children have wonderful insight into their own behavior and can offer great suggestions for improvement.

When you do need to intervene in a situation, it is important to watch where you put your focus. If your child pushes a sibling or a friend, it is instinctive to put our attention on the wrong-doer. Rather than focusing on the misbehavior, turn the situation around:

- Validate the child who was hurt. "I am so sorry that happened to you. I am sorry your feelings were hurt." Give a hug. "Let's swing together."

- Give the natural conscience time to work. Take the hurt child away with you, and let the child who did the pushing have time to consider her actions. She may be surprised that her pushing resulted in comfort and support to the other child.

- Revisit the issue at a time when both you and the child who did the misbehavior are calm. Read a book about being kind. Talk about the situation and what happened. Ask your child what she could have done instead to get what she needed. She will be in a frame of mind then to talk openly about what happened and ready to learn the deeper lessons of kindness.

- Role play. Rehearse positive, effective strategies. Then, when your child encounters a challenge again, remind her of the conversation and ask, "What steps did we talk about doing?" For example, "Your sister took the paints just as you were about to use them. What are some things we decided you can say?"

- Stay tuned in. Notice when your child solves the next challenge well. Immediately narrate what you saw working: "Thank you for being kind. You told Jane what you needed." Tuning in helps you direct your child's attention to appropriate resolutions and lets you celebrate her successes.

- Trust yourself and your knowledge of your child. You know your child best. If your child will respond well to an immediate quiet time on your lap talking about what happened, then take that approach. If it is better for your child to wait until later to talk about what happened, then do that. If your child wants to talk to you immediately because she needs help or comfort—and you are both calm—it is okay.

The primary goal is to become conscious of the ways you respond. Take every opportunity to build skills needed for healthy and positive behaviors. Use teachable moments to better understand what your children understand and believe and to encourage their progress. When you focus on the positive and shift to a skill-building mindset, you will find that parenting can be fun and fulfilling.

Seeing from Your Child's Point of View

My four-year-old daughter was enjoying her long bubble bath. She could have stayed in there all night. First, I said, "When you get out, then I will read a book." She snuggled down in the water and said, "I'm so warm."

Next, I held up the big bath towel in front of me and said, "Help! I am a sad, dry towel because I don't have a little girl to dry off." She scrambled out of the tub as fast as could be. I thought about all of the times I had gotten frustrated and demanded, "Get out. Get out." It was much easier to have fun, and she was proud to get out by herself.

Parents who focus on the positive find parenting joyful. This approach often requires thinking in a new way about how you respond to your children. Rather than stepping in afterward to correct behavior, consider all we can do ahead of time to set up children for success.

Of course children need reminders of your expectations, but there will come a time when your child says, "I know. I know. You don't have to remind me." This is a sign of growing maturity and shows that self-regulation has been internalized. Just smile and thank your child for being so responsible and taking care of things for herself: "It's awesome to be able to count on you!"

It is important to keep your perspective. There is a lot to learn. Your child's behavior and emotional regulation are still developing. Keep sight of the most important goals: shared time, enjoyment, a sense of humor, and comfort in being together. Following are additional ways to support success.

- **Keep looking ahead.** It is so much easier to step in early to redirect behavior than it is to react and try to fix a problem after it has already happened. When children are young, stay tuned in to their physical surroundings, and make sure to look ahead to anticipate potential problems.

- **Keep it simple.** When a child is balancing like a wild acrobat on her tricycle, avoid, "Oh my stars, you are going to fall down and crack your head open, and then I am going to have to call Aunt Millie to watch the baby and take you to the hospital." Simply say, "Feet on the pedals to be safe." When it is past time for bed, rather than warning, "You are going to be a tired mess and fall asleep tomorrow in school if you don't go to bed right now," say simply, "Bedtime." Not surprisingly, children listen to fewer words best!

- **Practice new skills.** Use the strategies in this chapter until you feel comfortable. These approaches may be used alone or combined as needed to invite cooperation and responsibility. Keep a journal so you can write what happened or lead up to an interaction, how you handled it, and how your child responded. Keep track of what works best.

- **Turn *no* into *yes* as often as possible.** When your child says, "May I go outside?" instead of saying, "No. Not now," try responding, "Yes. After lunch and nap, you may go outside to play." If she says, "I want to build a rocket ship," it might be tempting to say, "Not today. It will make a mess." Instead, you can respond, "That's a super idea. Let's collect the materials, and when Grandpa comes, he can help you build your design." Affirm and encourage great ideas.

- **Teach and practice simple manners.** "No, thank you." "Please may I have some?" "Thank you!" and "You're welcome!" are manners that never go out of style. Be sure to model these yourself. Before children leave the table or when they burp, "Excuse me" is appreciated. "Thank you for the nice time," will endear your child to others. Take time to teach manners, and make it fun.

- **Honor childhood.** What is important to you is not always important to your children. They are absorbed in play. You are absorbed in your responsibilities. Their imaginations are calling them to do something besides come to dinner. Their bodies are telling them to spin and roll and dance, just when you have a splitting headache and want quiet. They are doing all they can to please you, and they want to be competent. Be sure to affirm their world before asking them to join yours: "You have been having so much fun. I loved seeing you spin and dance. We need to go and get your brother in five minutes." "Your building is so colorful and interesting. I enjoy watching you put it together. I know you aren't finished, but we need to leave shortly." Stepping into their world first invites them to come back into yours and helps them feel honored and respected. You will see a remarkable difference in the way they respond to you.

You will gain keen understanding when you consider what an experience looks and feels like to your children. Do you make them feel safe? Do you help them be competent? Do you boost their confidence? Do you include them in your conversation? Do you show by your patience that you are glad they are here? A sense of security provides a rich soil for relationships and learning to grow.

CHAPTER 5
TEACHING
RESPONSIBILITY

Raising Helpers

I was at my sister's house when she asked my son to set the table. He was six at the time. I stepped in and said, "He has never done that before." My sister said, "Well, now is the time to teach him." I was so surprised by how much he enjoyed helping out. He offered to set the table every night that week.

A 2014 Pew Research Center study on parenting attitudes shows that the trait parents most desire for their children is responsibility. Almost all of those surveyed—93 percent—feel that teaching children to be responsible is especially important. Also included in the top three priorities are the qualities of hard work and helping others. To nurture these traits, begin with a mindset about caring and helping as a natural part of daily living.

There are many age-appropriate ways for children to pitch in and help. The idea is to start early and gradually build skills. Toddlers will love bringing a diaper when it's time for a change. It takes extra time, but letting your children help sort the silverware will feel like play to them. When they are in preschool and want to stack the cans, they will be so proud of their work and will spend their helping time talking with you. Shared tasks can be a regular and happy routine.

Helping is a natural desire that begins when children are very young. If you say yes to your toddler who wants to stand at the sink and help you rinse dishes, he will think helping is fun. If you say no and decide it's not worth the effort now when he is two, you may find it is not as easy to get him to help in the kitchen when he is three or four. Capitalize on early interest to set the pattern for the future.

Start small with simple tasks that you can do together: "It's such a happy time to have you hold the water sprayer for me. It makes dish time fun!" The laughter will shape your conversation as you get the chores done. Even a few minutes of fun at the sink will create positive emotions and connect pleasant feelings with doing the dishes. If you make helping enjoyable, the patterns will stick. One day, your child will be the kind of adult who makes the day happy for others, cheerfully pitching in to get needed tasks accomplished.

See if you can turn a chore into a challenge; a job into a game; a "must" into a "want to." Model pleasure in doing hard work.

Babies and toddlers watch to see how adults accomplish simple jobs. When you talk about what you are doing, they can learn how the world works: "Let's put the milk back in the refrigerator. Help me close the door." "Let's put the noodles in the orange bowl." "Daddy is putting in the filter for the coffee. Turn on the water. Let's pour the water into the pot." Taking time to describe each step does more than teach words. This daily exchange lights up your child's brain with new connections. The warm and safe feelings make thousands of neuron connections that create optimal learning—with an explosion of new language and understanding of concepts. Research by Susan Landry et al. supports the idea that positive affection, warmth, and sensitive responses encourage shared engagement during interactions and boost the development of language and learning.

In play, toddlers practice skills over and over. They put pegs in a plastic bottle and take them back out. They dump toys into a box and push it around. Dozens of times a day, they try on boots and shoes and comically march around. They balance plastic bowls on their heads as hats one minute and pour blocks in and out of a container the next. They imitate what they see adults do, each day strengthening needed dexterity and physical skills. By figuring things out for themselves, they make sense of how things work and satisfy their curiosity about how things happen.

Many toddlers are obsessed with sweeping floors. They love to throw things in the garbage by stepping on the foot pedal and watching the lid lift. They act out what they see adults do. Soon they will know how to coordinate their activities, placing objects in a wagon to take them where they need to go and chasing after balls that roll under chairs. Some parents call toddlerhood the "in and out" years, because children spend entire days putting objects in containers and taking them out again. In their daily activities, they are learning habits of thoughtfulness and self-reliance.

As your children grow, you can invite them to help complete simple chores such as folding laundry. Of course, children may roll in the clothes or sit inside the laundry basket to play instead of helping. Your patience will pay off as you truly enjoy laundry time together. Following are some ideas to make helping a natural part of every day.

- **Toddlers can help by**
    - ▶ throwing dirty clothes in a hamper or bucket, with a hearty cheer from you;
    - ▶ putting clothes in the washing machine or dryer and pushing the door shut;
    - ▶ bringing a diaper to you or helping put diapers away in the drawer or basket;
    - ▶ setting a cup or dish on the counter;
    - ▶ taking small items out of the dishwasher;
    - ▶ helping you put a few toys away;
    - ▶ carrying books to a shelf with assistance or putting them back into a basket while you hold it;
    - ▶ helping pick up bath toys by dropping them into a container before getting out of the tub; or
    - ▶ assisting as you take care of a pet.

- **Three- to five-year-olds can help by**
    - ▶ hanging a coat on a hook placed at the child's eye level;
    - ▶ stuffing mittens, gloves, and hats into a shelf or bin system;
    - ▶ wiping windows or dusting;
    - ▶ helping to wash, rinse, or dry dishes;

- using a squeegee in the shower after bathing;

- cleaning mirrors with a vinegar-and-water solution;

- walking the dog with you;

- pouring food or water in your pet's dish;

- folding and putting napkins next to plates;

- sectioning apples with a push-type apple corer, making a peanut-butter sandwich, spreading cream cheese on a bagel, measuring ingredients for recipes, or arranging simple food on a plate;

- helping pick up toys by putting like items back into a basket or shelf;

- sorting laundry into dark and light categories; or

- assisting with returning clean laundry to a shelf or drawer.

- **Five- to eight-year-olds can help by**

  - setting the table with adult supervision;

  - helping with food preparation with adult supervision;

  - cleaning or wiping out a pet cage, washing food bowls, pouring food or water into your pet's dish, and hanging up a leash;

  - collecting towels for the laundry;

  - bringing trash bins to be taken outside;

  - helping with laundry with adult supervision;

  - helping with yard work and household projects with adult supervision; and

  - vacuuming with adult supervision.

Responsibility for cleaning requires adult support. Teach the principle that being part of a family means taking care of your things and sharing in activities that matter to all of you. Be specific in the tasks you ask a child to do. If you say, "Go clean your room," the instruction is too broad and the child will feel overwhelmed. Instead, go with the child to his room and help understand what to do: "Let's pull the covers up and smooth out the blanket." "Let's put these dirty clothes in the hamper." "Let's put the stuffed animals in the basket." If you pitch in together, you can lighten the load and make daily living a pleasure instead of a chore.

One dad said, "I told my eight-year-old daughter, 'Let's make a plan to clean your room. What are some ways to get organized?' She said, 'I need to do my clothes and books.' So I said, 'Get all of your clothes into a pile. Put your toys in the bin. Then come and get me, and I will help you get the books arranged on your shelf.' Afterward, I helped her organize her closet." This kind of step-by-step plan works because a child feels like each step is manageable and understands that you are there to check in on his progress and help if needed.

Help your children see the benefit of taking care of their things. "It feels good to crawl into a clean bed at night." "Putting things back where they belong saves time in finding them the next time you need them." Focusing on the outcome helps children own the process rather than simply doing things because you tell them to.

Focus on process. "Keeping a liner in your waste basket helps, because then it is easy to carry down to the trash." "I am proud of the way you keep your school things. This is really helping you stay organized." "I am so happy to see how you arranged your collection. You are going to enjoy those for a long time." Compliment children when they make progress: "Your room stayed organized this week. What did you do to make that happen? It was fun to see you and Robbie playing together in there." When your children take time to be responsible, notice and let them know you care.

Be careful not to do for your children what they can do for themselves. Making them dependent on you isn't doing them a favor. Help them understand that pitching in is a natural part of being a family. Understanding that there is pride and benefit in taking care of things will prepare them to be happy and well-adjusted adults.

Enthusiasm is always contagious. One person with a cheerful heart and happy words can inspire cooperation from others. Working alongside a child is a great time to open up conversation. If you want to know what your child is thinking, join him in a task. When your children see the twinkle in your eye and know you will be making the job a pleasant time to share, they will look forward to doing it with you.

Using Words Wisely

I said to my five-year-old, "Em, you need to go back to bed!" Emily replied, "My eyes don't know how to sleep." The next morning, she climbed on my lap and said, "I just want to snuggle." I said, "I love snuggles with you. I love you. Do you love me?" She replied, "And Moo Moo (her stuffed animal)." This is the best part of parenting—the sweet and funny things children say when you least expect it.

Words are magic. They open a world of connection and communication with your child. Children who can share their ideas get the feedback of a parent's laughter and delight. Children who can talk out their feelings are less likely to act out their feelings. According to Eboni Howard, author of *What Matters Most for Children,* and Dana Suskind et al., authors of *Bridging the Early Language Gap,* children who have warm and interesting conversations with their parents do better in school—in every area. Language is the rocket fuel that propels children to higher levels of emotional under-standing, learning, communication, and healthy connection with others.

The way you think and talk to yourself guides your behavior and decisions hundreds of times throughout each day. This is true for children as well. Words help them talk to others to get what they need and talk to themselves to keep themselves on track. Words help them develop and keep strong friendships.

In talking with people you care about, you have to be intentional about your conversation and think about what will be interesting or memorable to the other person. There are many ways that you can boost the benefits of enriching language as you talk every day with your children.

- **Infants:**

  ► Nurture back-and-forth interactions. Tune in and respond when baby initiates. This lets him know that he can make good things happen and that he is important to you. He will find it funny when you mimic his sounds. This back-and-forth cooing and smiling is wiring his brain for language.

  ► Narrate what you are doing. "Daddy is picking you up and putting you into the high chair."

► Use descriptive words to talk about feelings. "I feel hungry. I can't wait to eat the strawberries." "I feel sad. Grandma had to go home." "You look tired. Let's go sit on the rocking chair."

► Narrate what the child is doing, "You put the big red block on the bottom. The yellow block is on top. What block will go next?"

► Talk about sounds and motion in the world. "Listen! Can you hear the airplane?" "Look. I see some birds."

► Talk about how you recognize emotion. "You have a beautiful smile. You look so happy." "That is funny! I like to laugh with you." "You are frowning. Are you sad?"

► Choose picture books with photos of real objects and everyday experiences. Point out the objects. A baby will be able to point before he can talk. "Where are the baby's eyes?" "Where is the kitten?" Until she can point independently, you point and give the answer for him. "There are the baby's eyes!" "There is the kitten!"

► Use fingerplays. Peekaboo, Eensy Weensy Spider, and How Big is Baby? will have your baby saying, "More!" in no time.

Making baby the center of your love and attention is the most important reason of all to enjoy these interactions.

• **Toddlers**

► Share positive feedback. "Good for you on fixing your car. You are a great problem solver."

► Focus on strengths. "You didn't give up! You made a good choice to move the chair out of your way."

► Describe emotions. "I can see you are sad. Let's hug teddy bear and read a book together." "I can see you got mad. Let's throw the bean bags into the bucket together." "We are happy Grandma is coming. Let's make a picture for her."

► Sing songs about emotions. Substitute other feeling words for the word *happy* in "If You're Happy and You Know It." Vary the tempo and change your tone of voice to match the emotion you are singing about.

▶ Make up stories to tell while driving or taking a walk. For example, tell a story about a mother bird you see who looks for food. Ask, "Where is the baby bird hiding?" "What did the mama bird feed her baby?"

▶ Encourage reading. Visit the library and find books with realistic drawings or pictures of real-life objects and activities. With your child, read multiple times daily in a comfortable place, making up conversations between characters in the book or describing what is happening in the pictures. Ask and then respond to your own questions until your child begins to point and respond independently. "What is the girl doing? She is kicking the ball to the dog." "The dog is running to get the ball. Where is the ball?" Point to the ball. "It rolled right under the tree!" Point to the tree. Your child will soon pick up a book to look at independently and will bring books to you to read together.

- **Pre-K and School-Age Children**

  ▶ Notice and describe positive actions. "Thank you for helping, Nolan. You are so kind." "How thoughtful of you to pick up your sister's books. She looks happy." "Thank you for looking out for Daniel and asking him to play. You are a good friend." Let children know that you notice and care that they contribute in positive ways to others.

  ▶ Focus on what children can do. "Will you show me what you did and tell me about it?" For older children, "I like your design. Will you explain how it works?" Focusing on process instead of the end result builds competence. Instead of, "That looks great," try, "I like how you made a pattern along the side."

  ▶ Read stories about children with specific feelings. Ask, "How did she feel?" "What would you feel?" "What did he do?" "What would you do?"

  ▶ Share creative art projects. Talk about emotions that are expressed in colors and patterns. Play music that enhances a mood. Creative arts connect children to expression of their feelings.

  ▶ Keep a feelings journal. Have your child dictate or write: "The happiest thing that happened to me today was . . ." "Something that made me mad today was . . ." "I wish you would . . ." "I wish that I could . . ." "I wish that I didn't have to . . ." "I wonder about . . ." Sentence starters invite authentic conversation about feelings that are important to children. As children get older, the habit of keeping a journal can become a wonderful and helpful tradition for them.

► Keep reading aloud. Older children love to listen to chapter books. Keep reading to them daily. Even when they begin to read aloud to you, continue reading to them, as well.

A song can help energize a child to pick up toys, go up the stairs, or complete a task. You may use a song you know or make up a singsong nonsense tune: "This is the way we brush our teeth, brush our teeth, brush our teeth. This is the way we brush our teeth early in the morning!" Singing adds a pop of rhythm, catches a child's attention, and encourages a positive attitude to start a routine or get a job done. It is one more way that you can enjoy words, rhymes, and rhythm with your children to keep their brains engaged and their spirits positive.

> Surprise the child by singing what you want him to do. Make up a song to a familiar tune, such as "The Wheels on the Bus," that describes what you are doing or what you want your child to do.

Talking about Emotions

When my son and daughter were at their doctor's appointment, I told the pediatrician they got along so well. I was mortified when, at that moment, they started kicking and screaming at each other.

Emotions are complicated! A person has to know how to identify what he feels before he can do something about it or talk about it. Sometimes it can be hard for an adult to recognize when he is upset. Children often need help in recognizing when they are upset, too. They can't use strategies for calming until they recognize that they are upset in the first place. A child may have a tight stomach, feel like hitting, want to cry, or feel anxious or sick. He needs to be able to notice and identify changes in his body and then distinguish between feeling disappointed, angry, out of control, or mad. That is a lot to do.

Because of the complexity of these tasks, children need adults to come alongside them to help them notice, name, and regulate their feelings. They need help to soothe their feelings; talk through what is happening; and share appropriate responses, such as hugging, rocking, deep breathing, or talking. Sensitive, responsive support is needed throughout childhood.

This shared process of support is called *coregulation of emotion* or *emotion coaching.* Children need adult help to navigate their own feelings and to understand the emotions of others. In fact, over a lifetime, a person often accomplishes emotion regulation inter-dependently rather than independently, as he seeks a friend to talk with, a shoulder to cry on, or even a pet to hug. Humans are remarkably interdependent, social beings.

Understand that your own emotions may be difficult to handle, and use this under-standing to be empathetic and patient with children. A child who is soothed and taught strategies for calming will more quickly calm himself and reach out for comfort rather than let his emotions spin out of control. He will learn to calm himself when he feels an upset feeling, before he acts on that feeling.

Helping children handle emotions is a priority. Be ready to nurture and support emotional competence in many ways—and remember that it takes a lifetime of practice to become mature.

- **Be ready with love.** Defuse intense emotions rather than confront the child. "I can see you are having a hard time. Let me give you a hug." Then, when the child is calm, you can talk quietly together about how to help.

- **Share soothing touch.** Physical skin-to-skin contact releases oxytocin and calms the stress response. Throughout the day, rub your child's hand, touch his arm, or scratch his back or neck. You will continue to be his favorite place to come when he needs comfort.

- **Give support.** Ask, "How can I help you?" "What can we do together to get what you need?" When a child hears this kind of caring response, it makes him open to cooperating.

- **Share calming strategies.** Model ways to calm down when you are feeling stressed or upset. "I am going to take a few deep breaths to calm down. I need to take a few minutes to think about what I want to do."

- **Focus on solutions.** "What do you need to solve the problem?" "What can we get that will help?" Caring words help children more quickly turn to problem solving.

- **Notice and point out when children handle emotions well.** "I am glad you told your sister you are frustrated." "I love to see you turn a boring moment into fun."

- **Change the environment.** Go for a walk in the neighborhood. Play in a sandbox or with water.

- **Introduce focus objects.** Try a squishy ball, a liquid timer, or thinking putty. Tactile sensations and calming sights can soothe upset feelings.

- **Visit a cozy space.** Create a cozy corner. Say, "I can see that you are breathing fast (or looking angry or making sounds of frustration). Why don't you take your blanket and pillow into the cozy corner until your body feels calmer?"

- **Play quiet music.** Say, "Help me put this song on. Then, we can snuggle on the couch and listen."

- **Introduce art activities.** Sensory touch is soothing. Fingerpainting in shaving cream, painting or drawing on large paper, or making an outline of the child's body on paper are all ways to refocus emotional energy and calm the body.

- **Read books.** There are so many children's books that introduce and talk about children's experiences and emotions in sensitive ways. See the list of recommended children's books on page 191 for suggested materials.

- **Watch a soothing video.** For older children, it can be calming to watch an orchestra, a slow-paced wildlife film, or a video of nature.

Feeling empathetic to others, showing forgiveness or compassion, recognizing and managing anger in a productive way, coping with disappointments, and taking responsibility for feelings without blaming others can be very challenging. It helps to think about how much adults have to work at these skills. This perspective will help you to remain patient as your children learn to handle their own complex emotions.

Model how to be responsible for your feelings and actions: "I was impatient and snatched the remote control away. I am sorry." Soon children will learn to own their emotions. "I was angry and took his toy. I am sorry." "I was mean to Ryan and took his truck." Taking time to talk about what has happened shows children that emotions are an important part of relationships. Owning our actions and words take practice and patience.

Helping Children Become Self-Controlled

As described by the Harvard Center on the Developing Child, the traffic-control center of the brain includes a group of skills called *executive function*. These skills include the ability to shift and focus attention. Executive function helps activate energy to get started, yet also helps delay gratification or inhibit action. Executive function helps a person remember what she needs to do, through *self-talk*—the words we say to ourselves to direct our behavior, making lists, or planning a calendar. These skills help a person regulate his emotions and calm himself when he feels upset or anxious. Teaching responsibility for time, body, emotions, belongings, and personal space is a big task. Recognizing the ways these skills work together can help you become more thoughtful about the kind of support you give to your child.

Building Independence

My son was five and having meltdowns every morning about his clothes. I got a hanging shelf that was made as a shoe organizer. We marked each slot by day, Monday through Friday, and put his clothes in the slots for each day. After that, he was able to get dressed on his own.

"Do it myself!" is the chant of most three-year-olds. However there is a lag between the desire for independence and the physical ability to carry out a task. There is a learning curve as children become more coordinated, practice skills, and get comfortable with procedures. Stay sensitive to what your child can do alone at each age, and give needed support for the things he wants to try to do.

Often children arrive at school and teachers wonder why parents are still zipping coats and tying shoes when children can do it for themselves. Ask your child's teacher what the expectations are, so that you can teach and reinforce these skills at home. This will be a huge boost to your child's competence when he faces the social and physical expectations and requirements of other settings. Your support in the development of needed skills can minimize your child's frustration.

Step in ahead of time and aim for success in every interaction. This doesn't mean that you should swoop in at every sign of struggle. Children need time and space to figure things out for themselves. Give children time to become flexible and adept at thinking of new ways to work things out. Notice what works well and what needs to be revisited and supported. And don't let your child become discouraged.

Ask children to help with real-life problems. "We didn't handle coming in for dinner very well. I wonder what we can do next time." "Where's a good place to park your bike in the garage?" By putting the child in charge, he will be more willing to take ownership of the outcome. It is amazing how creative and thoughtful children are when given a chance to offer their ideas.

Children need to grow competence over time in facing age-appropriate challenges while managing the natural frustrations. When a bike tips over, a foot gets stuck in a boot, or a drink spills, reorienting and managing situations independently takes practice. Following are some kinds of independence you can support, as appropriate for the children's ages and abilities:

- Taking care of their own things: putting away toys, gathering books for school, hanging up coats

- Helping others: bringing in the mail, walking the dog, watering the flowers, setting the table

- Doing tasks in the kitchen: peeling a banana, opening a yogurt cup, pouring juice

- Getting dressed and putting pajamas in the hamper

- Tying their own shoes

- Taking clothes to the bedroom

- Rehearsing expectations for school

- Visiting friends

- Getting ready for sports or lessons

- Staying organized

> Tell children frequently, "You have a good head on your shoulders. You decide. I trust your judgment. What do you think you can do?"

Children often come running to an adult for help or assistance. Sometimes it is faster or easier to make decisions for them and answer their questions right away instead of asking what they can do. But children need, with your support, to shift the focus to their own problem-solving and thinking skills. Support their growing skills, and then encourage them to decide on options for themselves.

Motivating Effort

My husband was with the children, raking and talking with the neighbor children. They stopped to jump in the piles of leaves. Soon the bags were stuffed and lined up. They came in yelling, "We're done!" I was so proud that they worked so hard.

As reported by Liana Heitin in *Education Week* and according to research by Jean Twenge and Keith Campbell, American children are ranked highest in self-esteem but much lower in academic performance. This means that even when they feel great about themselves, they may not have the skills to back up their goals. There is a gap between a can-do attitude and the determination and hard work needed to succeed.

Ashley Merryman, coauthor of *Top Dog: The Science of Winning and Losing*, says it's not so great to be the best. Overinflated praise leads children to avoid challenges. Children need to learn to work hard to earn success and to gain competence. Overpraising does not raise self-esteem and can actually reduce motivation. Researcher Carol Dweck points out that children who are praised often and given rewards will engage less carefully so that they can hurry to finish. Rather than simply offering praise, it is better to talk about what worked well and why. Focusing on the process helps children work more thoughtfully.

Children need to learn to lose gracefully, to take the smaller portion, to wait their turn. To raise well-balanced children, you have to teach them to handle difficulties as well as successes and to know how to handle disappointments. Learning how to lose and fail is an important life lesson.

Learning to work hard and be happy will come through your example. If you don't complain but pitch in to work with a positive approach, your children will learn to do the same. Be careful not to praise children for simply doing what they ought to be doing.

Teach your children to follow the directions of trusted adults. Teach them how something should be done. There are procedures and rules they will need to follow. In a world of do-it-yourself creativity, children still need knowledge and skills to know how to participate with others. They need the trait of persistence.

Self-efficacy is the power of believing you can, the ability to define a desired goal and to see oneself as capable of reaching that destination. Children need to believe that their effort is worth it. Self-efficacy fuels their ongoing motivation to keep on trying and to invest positively in helping themselves and others.

Motivation is the ability to get oneself going, to actively initiate behavior. Motivation will help a person persist in the face of difficulty and work hard toward a goal. Sometimes parents say, "My child just isn't motivated." This implies that motivation comes within the child, when, according to researcher Judit Szente, it is highly dependent on what children need and receive from us. What makes children step up and engage in tasks with effort and persistence? Verbal persuasion matters. "You can do it!" Those are powerful words. Children also feel more motivated when they have a personal interest in a subject, value an activity, or are solving a personal challenge. They are highly motivated when they have some choice and control over decisions. They will engage eagerly when they feel competent. Current success builds ongoing motivation. Following are ways to use feedback to boost children's competence:

- **Managing emotions:** "Even though you got frustrated, you tried again to balance the blocks." Name the emotion, and describe what the child did to regulate that emotion and his response to it.

- **Persistence:** "You did so well organizing the books, because you kept working at it even when they toppled over." Name what was accomplished and why it worked out.

- **Independence:** "Awesome! You worked hard to match all of the letters tiles by yourself!" Focus on the independent work, rather than on whether the child got the correct answers.

- **Self-regulation:** "How kind! You helped George zip his coat, even when you wanted to run and play." Name what the child did and how he delayed gratification.

- **Initiative:** "Three cheers! You picked up the toys from the floor without being asked. Now it is easier for me to walk by." Name the action and the benefit to self or others.

- **Strategy:** "When you cleaned your room, you started with a really good plan and followed it. Step by step, you got it done." Describe what worked well.

- **Problem solving:** "How wonderful that you and Madison decided how to share the dolls! You are good problem solvers." Or, "Can you help me decide where to put this? You are a good problem solver." Describe the action and link it to good choices.

- **Resolving conflict:** "Thank you for coming to tell me and for using your words instead of hitting or hurting someone." Describe what you saw. Ask the child how he can address the issue or how you can work something out together.

- **Creativity:** "What a unique solution to your problem. Your thinking was very creative." Help the child perceive himself as capable.

Most parents want their children to know that no one else in the world is just like they are and that being original is fantastic. But you also want them to enjoy the challenge of hard work and to gain a strong sense of determination and the willingness to overcome obstacles. These traits will prepare them well for life ahead.

Encouraging Self-Direction

I got tired of nagging at my first and second graders about putting their books in their backpacks for school. Homework wasn't a much prettier picture. I asked them how they can remember their school things. They came up with two questions they have to ask each other: "Do I have my lunch?" "Do I have my books?" When I gave the responsibility to them, they used the steps and remembered.

When children are small, they are completely dependent on adults for everything. From the moment they wake up until they are tucked in at night, they need constant attention. To shift the responsibility from yourself to your child over time, you need a plan. By the end of the eighth year, a child should have a reliable level of competence in each area of self-care and personal responsibility. Intentional planning can make that happen.

Aim to help your child become self-directed. Ask him to help you. "What are the best ways of getting this done?" "What are my options here?" "How can I do this that will work the best?" Children have a lot to say, and we can learn from their ideas.

When children hear, see, and practice responsible choices, they learn how to make good decisions for themselves. Give your child intentional guidance. "When you were little, I took care of everything for you. Now that you are bigger, you can decide. Would you rather do your homework now, or would it work better for you to do it after you play in the back yard for a bit?" Build up your child with your words. Help him learn to problem solve and find best ways of directing his own behavior. Some children will respond, "I want to do it now and get it out of the way." If the child does choose to go outside, be sure to ask, "How long do you want to be outside?" Then, set the timer and send it out with the child. The timer also transfers the responsibility to the child.

> Help your child brainstorm possible solutions to a dilemma, problem, or predicament. "What is a good plan of action?" "What would happen if you solved it that way?" Model your own thinking steps, as your child can learn how to brainstorm from you.

The more specific you are about helping your child think about needed steps, the better. Following are strategies that, over time, will help your child become happily self-directed.

- **Ask instead of tell.** This approach puts the child in charge of his own behavior and helps him be thoughtful about his actions:
    - ▶ Instead of "Use your words," ask, "What do you say when you don't like something?"
    - ▶ Instead of "Stop touching her," ask "How do you feel when someone is in your space?"
    - ▶ Instead of "Get down from the chair," ask, "Where does your body need to be?"
- **Narrate what works.** Notice when things are going well, and point out the reasons or strategies:
    - ▶ "You are doing a great job keeping your hands and feet to yourself."
    - ▶ "That is a great choice to bring a book with you."
    - ▶ "Good for you to curl up for a few minutes and calm down."
    - ▶ "When you got stuck, you went around your brother without bumping his puzzle."

- **Prompt success.** Keep the focus forward to ensure a positive outcome.

  ▶ "Yes, you can run around before dinner, but you need to do it outside or in the basement."

  ▶ "The papers need to go in the basket. Do you need my help to straighten them out, or can you do it by yourself?"

There will be times when you have to say, "I need you to do your homework now, because we have to go out later. Would you like to do it at the coffee table or on the kitchen table?" When you look at a situation long term, you can see how self-control is the goal. Self-control is self-sustaining and becomes easier over time. Eventually, you want your children to remember to do their homework on their own. When you are short on time, it may feel easier to give orders and make children comply. If you do, there are short-term benefits but long-term drawbacks. If you consistently give back responsibility, children will step up to figure out things for themselves. You can help them brainstorm solutions, and over time they will learn what works best.

Inviting Creativity

My son was eighteen months old when he first heard the trumpet played at his cousin's camp. He said, "Mommy, I want to do that." We bought some jazz CDs and took him to hear jazz in the park. His interest stuck, and he started taking lessons when he was eight.

The best way to nurture your child's gifts and talents is to notice what he loves to do. To encourage music creativity, for example, share your own love of music, dance together, and sing. Play musical games using different voices and copycat clapping or tapping rhythms. Expose children to concerts in the park and children's symphony events. Enjoy musicals together. Listening to different kinds of music boosts interest.

Light up your child's interest as you choose library books about the topic he is interested in. Try engaging in the interest with your child. If he loves to draw and paint, set aside time to do this together. Create a display space on your refrigerator or a bulletin board to showcase his explorations. If he loves to dance, dance with him to different types of music. Children will often open up and talk while they are exploring music, movement, and art. These times of shared exploration can create lasting memories of closeness and conversation.

If you want your child to take lessons, arrange a trial lesson first. If you have questions, request a time to talk with the school or teacher when your child is not present. Find out what is expected and consider whether your child is really ready and wants to participate. Before the age of eight, the goal is to follow the child's interest and desire and to make creativity fun. Be sure practice times are short, positive, and consistent. Music and art that bring a child joy can become life-long passions.

If a school-aged child asks to start lessons or a creative activity, he should see these through—at least to the end of the semester or season. It is important that children learn to be responsible in finishing what they start. It takes effort and determination to keep at a skill. Sticking with something and getting through the hard parts can reward a child with satisfaction.

> Think ahead about whether the child is capable of handling the situation. Be realistic, and remember to focus on the child's needs, not just your own agenda.

Whether participating in classes, lessons, or enjoying creativity at home, the benefits to your child are enormous. As researchers Sylvain Moreno et al. and Rebecca Parlakian and Claire Lerner have asserted, music and the arts nurture awareness of the self and others. They foster thinking skills, persistence, and self-regulation. Throughout the school years, the arts will introduce your child to good friends and happy experiences with others. The arts are the universal language that can open a world of exploration and future adventure for your child.

Nurturing Gifts and Talents

When my first child turned one, I thought, "I can take some credit for this sweet personality." Then my second child turned out to be twins, and each one had a distinct personality. Both were rambunctious and funny. Then we had our fourth child, and he was neat as a pin—just came into the world lining things up and organizing everything. When he was one, he would take off his shoes and put his socks inside all by himself. That's when I realized I could influence their spirits, but their personalities were a built-in feature.

An important goal of parenting is to discover and nurture your children's gifts. Foster their passion for science or reading or cooking—whatever it is they enjoy. There are other traits, such as a sense of humor, flexibility, and determination, which are just as important as natural ability.

At first, you may focus on getting your baby clean, feeding him, finding clothes that fit, and praying he sleeps through the night. Those first few months are about learning the patterns and getting a grip on all of the new skills you need. Then, you gaze at that sweet face as he lies angelically in the crib, and you wonder what he'll be like when he gets older.

By age two, children often have charming personalities and a knack for dancing and making a mess. By age three, their favorite activity is doing what you are doing. By five, they may have developed an obsession with building or painting. Maybe they are so messy that you despair of having a clean home ever again, until you realize that, perhaps, they are creative. A mom of three children said, "I bought my five-year-old daughter a t-shirt that read, 'I am not messy. I am creative.' And she really was. I figured she would grow out of the messy room, but I wanted to nurture her creative spirit. I am glad I chose to do it that way."

Another mom said, "My daughter was so intense about her activities that she would work on a project or scenario for days. Sometimes I would sneak in at night and help her get organized so that she would wake up in the morning and think it was a dream, like *The Little Princess*. By the time she was eight, she turned the corner and became obsessed with arranging things. But when we started out, I just told her she was my creative princess. I am glad I made her feel loved and didn't scold for all of the wonderful projects she got started in her room, often leaving a mess with fabric, costumes, and art."

Daniel Pink, the author of *A Whole New Mind: Why Right-Brainers Will Rule the Future*, says, "The future belongs to a very different kind of person with a very different kind of mind—creators and empathizers, pattern recognizers and meaning makers. These people—artists, inventors, designers, storytellers, caregivers, consolers, big-picture thinkers—will now reap society's richest rewards and share its greatest joys." With vast changes in the workforce, children will need adaptive skills to solve problems and collaborate with others, and will need to employ a set of strategic skills and strengths that rely on divergent thinking and creativity.

As your children explore new interests, try to accept the messes that might be made along the way, be ready for the lessons learned by trial and error, and nourish your children's freedom to bloom. Your job is to help them discover the gifts they bring into the world and to find ways to help these grow. Let them know the joy of doing something that is satisfying and useful.

Some days, children will be brilliant and amazing. Other days, they may show no interest at all in an activity. This is perfectly normal. Notice the times they are being creative, and encourage them in the process.

No matter what your child's interests and gifts, remember that over time these interests may shift and other talents may develop. It is normal for a four-year-old to love gymnastics but to switch to an obsession with sewing when he is eight. Be sure to keep your own passions alive so that you find your deepest satisfaction in being yourself—rather than living through your child. Focus on encouraging responsibility, and have fun together.

> Accept children's strengths and weaknesses, seeing them for who they are and letting it be okay. Don't put on them what they cannot live up to, but nurture their individual gifts and talents.

CHAPTER 6
UNDERSTANDING THE BOUNCE-BACK FACTOR— RESILIENCE

Defining Resilience

I took my daughter on a daddy-daughter date. The car broke down, and we were stuck on the side of the road. We waited for the tow truck, and she rode with me to the gas station. I was so worried that she was having an awful time, but we made it into an adventure. At the end of the day, she told me it was the best day she had ever had.

The words of wisdom that experienced parents share at a baby shower don't always translate into practical advice when children are fighting on a long road trip. You may have another three hours and are completely out of ideas. In those harried moments, you may notice your heart pounding and wonder if you are really cut out for parenting. You want to handle this challenge well, so you make a conscious choice to interrupt the frustration you feel as your three-year-old screams, "Stop!" at her brother for hitting her across the seat. Instead of yelling, you gather your wits and muster the determination to stay calm. You pass back a book, turn up the music, and stay positive. Ultimately, you know that you can't teach them to manage daily frustrations if you can't handle them yourself.

Life is full of ups and downs and experiences that do not go the way you want them to. Understand the remarkable power of your influence to help children handle stress, and learn to respect and nurture them and yourself with love. Understanding how to reorient during daily pressures is an important life skill.

Resilience is the ability to bounce back, recover, and thrive in spite of frustrations. It helps children reorient more quickly when they face struggles and look for alternatives when they face disappointments. Instead of giving up, resilience gives an inner drive to make things work out. Resilient children seek help when needed, stay optimistic, and keep a sense of humor. They handle upsets by being flexible and creative, and they use all available resources to make the most out of each situation.

Resilience benefits you, too. You want to show kindness and calm when you feel upset. You want to handle your own life in constructive and adaptive ways. If you live and model these traits, your children will understand that figuring things out and moving on are a part of life. This realization can help you find renewed determination and patience as you recognize what a gift you are passing on to your children.

Not only do children pick up your words and actions, they also internalize the emotional patterns of your life. If they see you respond impulsively, lose your temper, or get frustrated, they wonder if things will be okay. They worry how they will be able to cope, because they don't see you coping well. This anxious undercurrent makes them hold on more tightly to ineffective choices rather than let go and look for a plan of action that will work better.

You can nurture resilience when you stay positive and show your children how to look out for others as well as themselves. Show what rebounding looks and feels like, so that your children can move confidently forward through each day.

Managing Risks

It is instinctive to want to protect children from stress. You may try to shield them from worry and keep them from witnessing disturbing events. The inborn desire is to guard them from physical and psychological trauma. Some risks are necessary as children learn how to watch out for themselves. They need to experience physical challenges, such as scrambling up a stone wall, climbing trees, and exploring nature. They learn to balance personal with social time, choose friends, explore new relationships, and satisfy their curiosity about the world around them. Each of these challenges presents tolerable risk—risk that helps children learn and thrive. Rather than try to control everything that happens, help each child become a successful explorer, creator, investigator, and designer of her own happy experiences.

When stress is brief and a natural part of reaching new milestones, children learn that they can handle the challenge. But when patterns of stress develop, the impact can be detrimental. Ongoing stresses of a more serious nature can be harmful and even toxic. It is important to evaluate children's exposure to stress. If you see changes in sleep or behavior patterns or notice signs of anxiety such as clinging or acting out, try to identify potential stressors and provide relief or support.

In a poll of parents of children ages birth to age three, which was conducted on behalf of Zero to Three, two-thirds said they did not realize that infants are affected by arguing or the stress of adults around them. In fact, research shows that when young children witness arguing, yelling, or tension between their parents or caregivers, the effect on their bodies is the same as if the anger were aimed directly at them. Ongoing parental anger causes a child's cortisol levels to rise. Cortisol is a hormone produced by the adrenal gland. It is a natural response to stress and is sometimes called the "fight or flight" hormone. However, ongoing elevated cortisol levels can have damaging effects on a child's brain development and health, according to the National Scientific Council on the Developing Child at Harvard University. Children need reassurance and comfort to handle stress, particularly if that stress is ongoing, and they rely on the stability and security of their parents or other adult caregivers. If you find that your own patterns of tension are more than temporary, seek support or counseling that can help you find healthier ways to resolve issues.

- In the findings of the 2009 Zero to Three survey, only 30 percent of parents said they knew that children can experience sadness and fear by six months of age.

- One in five parents thought children can control their emotions, such as not having a tantrum when frustrated, by two years of age.

- Only 34 percent of parents knew that infants and toddlers can sense if parents are angry or sad and can be affected by these moods. In fact, parental depression is a risk factor for children. If you suffer from depression, or have a partner who does, discuss the matter with a pediatrician, so that your children and you can receive needed support.

Young children are particularly vulnerable to stress in the relationships of others closest to them. According to *InBrief: The Impact of Early Adversity on Children's Development*, published by the Center on the Developing Child, adverse stress experienced in early childhood can influence mental and physical health later in life. Young children are not able to cope with stress in the same way that adults do. Their emotions, understandings, and capacity to manage have not fully developed. But, as long as the stress is short term within a secure environment of responsive adults, children can be resilient.

All of us need to support each other and the children in our lives, noticing and caring when we see difficulties and reaching out for professional guidance when needed. You can build a nurturing and caring support system around yourself and your children.

Gaining Strength from Difficulty

"Cat! Oh no! We have hit a cat!" The words came flying out of my aunt's mouth before she could hold them in, and her reaction scared the children in the back seat of the car. My four-year-old daughter started to cry. We did our best to soothe her, but she had lingering cat dreams for several months afterward.

No matter how much you plan, the unexpected will happen. Even the most loving parents experience moments where their own stress or shock leaves an indelible impression on young observers. Your consistent support can help move your children beyond a traumatic event, but when children are emotionally sensitive, a memory can be lasting.

A mom shared, "We were visiting a friend of my mother's when my daughter picked up a puppy from a basket. It wiggled out of her hands and tumbled down the stairs. Even though the puppy was okay, my daughter still remembers the upset reaction of the woman. Several years have passed, but she is still afraid to pet a dog."

When children are upset or in the middle of an emotional crisis, you need to ensure safety for their feelings. If a parent or caregiver is overdramatic and fills the space with their own anxiety and worry, children may respond by internalizing rather than expressing what they feel. Reassurance that you can handle your children's emotions and that you will remain stable when they talk to you shows them that feeling upset is not earth shattering. They need to know that intense feelings will pass, and that you are there to help them when they need you.

- **Set everything aside.** Tell your children often that when they need to talk, you will put everything aside and listen. When children are going through stressful times, be ready when they need a hug and available when they need to talk.

- **Be a safe place.** Children may be afraid to share their feelings. Reassure them: "You can tell me when you are afraid." "I won't be upset if you are mad." "You will not get into trouble. I will not be mad at you if you tell me something you see or hear." "There are no silly questions." A good time to give these reminders is when things feel calm and secure.

- **Teach words to ask for help.** Children need to know how to ask for help: "I need to talk." "Something happened . . ." Tell them that it takes courage to ask for help for ourselves or for others.

- **Empower inner strength.** Affirming children's strengths teaches them to trust their feelings and perceptions. "You are wise to think of that." "It is true what you say. You explained it very well." "You are very empathetic to notice he was feeling that way." "You have a good sense about people's feelings."

When a significant change has taken place in a child's life, you may wonder if you can give the kind of support that will compensate for the challenge. Some events happen for a brief period and then life returns to normal. Other events have a lasting impact. The most important factor in your child's ability to recover is a close and secure connection with you and with other caring adults.

> "You are caring and kind." "You are good at figuring things out!" These comments focus attention on the traits that lead to happy and healthy outcomes.

Often children develop a special empathy for others, because they remember how it felt when something happened to them. One mom shared, "My son was hospitalized when he was two for a broken ankle, and he suffered other health issues. Now that he is six, he still shows a remarkable kindness and empathy to others."

Children must balance upsetting memories with the security they receive through positive family and school experiences. It is comforting to know that often in the greatest challenges are found life lessons that can help your children become more caring and invested in the lives of others. Challenges and difficulties are part of the life experiences that provide inspiration for our passions.

Seeing Things as They Are

My children told their aunt about our trip to the park. I remembered it as being fun, but they remember me getting mad. It's funny how I didn't remember the whole story.

An important responsibility of parenting is to affirm what is true. In *The Truth Will Set You Free,* author Alice Miller calls this the role of the "enlightened witness." Instead of minimizing or skipping over the child's feelings, an enlightened witness affirms what is true. For example, a six-year-old says, "I remember when you got mad at the store lady." Rather than say, "I wasn't mad, Jack. It wasn't that bad," his mom can say, "Yep. That was a super-hard day, and I am sorry I lost my temper. I felt sorry about it afterward." If Dad has moved out as part of a separation and your child says, "I feel sad about Daddy," rather than reply, "It's okay. You are going to visit him this weekend at the park," you can say, "I understand, Emma. Mommy feels sad, too. But we are going to keep having special times with Daddy, and you can talk to him every day."

Being able to see and experience the world accurately is a building block of resiliency. Children need an adult who listens and affirms the truth of their perceptions. "Did I do something to make Daddy mad?" "Was I the cause of that frustration?" Parents can help children put their feelings into words. "Yes, Daddy got super mad. He went to take a walk so that he could calm down. You didn't do anything wrong, and he will talk with us again when he comes home. I am sorry that was upsetting." It is not easy to take responsibility for what's going on or to honestly admit what is happening.

If you pretend that nothing happened, children will internalize a strong message that it is better not to talk about struggles. You want the opposite to happen. Children need to feel safe coming to a caring adult. "When you are afraid or worried, you can tell me. I promise to answer your questions." This simple invitation given throughout childhood opens the door for honest communication. By really listening and affirming the truth, you nurture trust.

Children may say, "I don't like that you did this," or "You don't listen to me." Rather than defend yourself, you can say, "I am so glad you told me that. I can understand why you feel that way." Even very young children know when we are distracted. When they are fussy or upset, you can say, "I understand why you are crying. I would cry, too, if my diaper was dirty. Let's go get you changed." "I am sorry I was so busy. I know that's disappointing. I'll put my phone away so that we can spend time together." Your ability to stay emotionally available and be a witness to the truth really matters. You are building a pattern of honesty that will make all the difference in the teen years and beyond.

When you are sensitive to your children, they will stay sensitive to themselves and others in return. When little brother is crying, it's important to say to an older child who is near, "I feel sad that Caleb is crying. I am going to comfort him." If you ignore the crying, another child may not understand that the distress is not due to pain or that the baby is not doing anything wrong. Rather than ignore emotional cues, talk about them. "Caleb is tired, but he'll be asleep in a few minutes. I will read to you when I finish putting him to sleep." The ability to identify, understand, and respond to your own and others' emotions is an essential key for resilience.

> Allow children to want what they want and feel what they feel. Don't try to talk them out of or feel guilty for their wants and needs. "It's okay to feel sad. Let's sit together and talk about it." "I know you are disappointed. It's hard to wait when we want something."

Having someone acknowledge their feelings helps children release them and move forward. Children want and need to know that you understand how they feel. Naming their emotions and saying "It's okay!" is reassuring and takes the air out of the resistance balloon. Rather than try again and again to convince us of their wants and needs, a child who feels heard is able to shift mentally and to focus on other options and solutions.

Intervening in Teasing and Bullying

> *My son is only three, and another child is mean to him at child care. I told him that the only words that matter are the ones that the people who love him say.*

Children face social conflict at an incredibly young age. When children are toddlers, they are not yet programmed to share. This is not because they are selfish, as they love to do things for others. It is because they are still in a parallel-play stage, in which they play next to rather than with others, and are focused solely on their own activity. Their world is still egocentric, meaning that they are involved in their own physical sensations, feelings, and interests. They are just learning to be aware of what is around them and to see and understand the perspectives or needs of others. This is a developmental stage and needs to be supported and respected. Toddlers need constant supervision to be sure they are safe and do not take out their frustrations through hitting or biting. Soon they will be able to use words to express frustrations and ask for what they need.

From the ages of three to five, children need adult support to work out disagreements. By age six or seven, they begin to exhibit jealousy and can make comments that are unkind. "Her hair is ugly." "She is not your friend. She is just pretending to like you." Take these issues seriously, and be active in teaching and reinforcing kindness. Be ready to intervene. If your child says, "My feelings got hurt," you can say, "That would hurt my feelings, too. I wouldn't want someone saying that to me, either." Restating and validating the feelings is an important step in helping your child let them go.

At times, squabbles and teasing can turn into a prolonged issue of bullying. In bullying, a child causes physical or emotional pain by exerting power, fear, or social pressure to make another child feel bad. Sometimes, bullies are children who themselves have been bullied. They take out their feelings of unworthiness or lack of empowerment on others. However, it is important to accept that many children feel pressured to tease and bully because of the desire to be accepted by peers. Often, those who bully are known to be socially competent, good looking, and smart. They are often well-liked and respected children. So no one rule applies.

Many people do teach their children about bullying—assuming that their child will be the victim but never the bully. That oversight can prevent parents from helping their children in the way that they most need. Every child may at some time become an aggressor. When you notice your child taking out anger on, picking on, or bullying another child, don't assume the behavior will go away on its own or that your child will grow out of it. Instead, intervene immediately. Talk about the experiences that are prompting the feelings of anger or aggression. Perhaps a child struggles with jealousy and needs reassurance. It may be that a child is feeling hurt, angry, or lonely and is directing those feelings outward. Be sure to say, "I will not let someone else hurt you, and I cannot let you hurt someone else. It is okay to feel angry, but it is never okay to hurt someone else." Then you can make it a priority to read books about children's emotions that are similar to your child's feelings. Encourage your child to tell you when she is frustrated or angry rather than to retaliate or become physical with another child. The good news is that all children can learn new ways of handling anger and resolving conflicts and can benefit from training about empathy and kindness.

Start when children are young, and tell them to get help, both when they are being teased or bullied and when they feel like teasing or bullying others. Every child can find herself in a situation she does not know how to handle. You can teach the following steps:

> Empower children by role-playing. Help them practice speaking up and getting help when needed. Point out positive role models who show empathy and caring to others.

- **Get help.** When someone is mean or hurtful, walk away and get help. Walk away if you feel like being mean or hurtful.

- **Speak up.** When you are being teased or bullied, try saying loudly, "I don't like that!" or "Please stop." If the teasing or bullying continues, get help right away.

- **Help your friend.** When a friend is being hurt, ask him to walk away with you, and get help together.

Teasing and bullying most often involve a power imbalance, such as three children ganging up on another child, or a child who is larger, stronger, or has a more dominant personality intimidating a weaker or shyer child. Therefore, adults need to be active in intervention. Here are the steps to take:

- **Validate.** The adult should validate the child's feelings. "Thank you for telling me. I am sorry your feelings were hurt." "I am sorry that happened."

- **Problem solve.** Help the child—or group of children—problem solve. "What do you think you could do to work it out?" However, be cautious, as a child may suffer retaliation for getting help. It is often better to monitor the situation so that you witness it yourself. "I will keep an eye on this, so that if it happens again, I will step in."

- **Monitor carefully.** Be ready to intervene immediately when you see a child being physically hurt or threatened. "I am sorry. I cannot let you hurt others. It is my job to keep you all safe." Children who have begun a pattern of hurting others need to know that adults will step in to ensure safety.

- **Build trust.** Help children look for and compliment positive traits in each other. This can build trust, even with a peer who might otherwise be negative. Be sure to focus on noticing and drawing attention to positive traits in your own child, as well.

Talk with children individually and together about what they experience. Give them an open door to come to you. However, if a pattern continues, it is important to get others involved. Below are the steps to take to involve other parents:

- Reassure other parents that you want the very best for all of the children. Share the idea that anyone's child can tease or bully and all need to work together.

- Agree to step in and support children—before things get out of hand.

- Ensure a culture of kindness. Remind all children that words can hurt, but kindness can help—and that you trust them to be caring with others.

- Talk often with other parents, and work together to ensure safety. Children need to know that your messages to them are the ones that are true, and that unkind words are not the truth. They need to know that you are watching and that you will keep them safe. Stay vigilant and be ready to intervene.

Handling Failure

My twins tried out together for soccer because their older brother played. One of them was devastated when he didn't make it but his twin brother did. He cried and was really sad about it. His brother tried to make him feel better. In the end, we talked about how everyone has different strengths and he could try again or try something else.

Teach your children that life is not always fair and tough challenges will come their way. Help them find strategies that will work when things go wrong, and teach them to not give up. Every day, mishaps can happen and disappointments will come.

A mom related, "My eight-year-old daughter auditioned for the elementary-school play and really wanted to be Dorothy. She was devastated when she didn't get any part at all. After one night of being upset, she decided to help out with the stage design and ended up having a blast painting sets and working with her friends.

It may be that a child who doesn't make a sports team will try something new. Perhaps the loss will make her determined to keep working on her skills and try again. Sometimes, a child needs to choose, and other times you need to steer her gently to discover new interests. Importantly, you can teach children that challenges are opportunities to grow. You can help them evaluate their options and weigh the benefits of trying again—and trying new experiences. The wisdom they gain through failing teaches important life lessons and provides them with insight to apply to future experiences.

Navigating Times of Change

We've had everything from bad weather to another job change. I am trying my best, but I worry about how to help our children handle the stress.

Many people experience times when unforeseen stresses impact their families. Having a plan of action in mind can help children adjust to a move, the loss of a pet, coping with a parent away for an extended time, or parental job insecurity. There are many ways to help children adjust and thrive.

One caring mom said, "Kyle got really angry when we moved. He was only four when we arrived at the new house. He marched around and said, 'I hate it. I hate it. Where will I ride my bike? This is a stupid house.' He stayed mad for a long time, and nothing we said would console him. He missed the basement of our old house where he spent hours riding his bike indoors."

It is common for families to move and for children to say goodbye to a beloved friend, family member, or home. Following are some ideas for smoothing the transition of a move:

- Create a special notebook for family and friends to write a brief letter or include a picture for the child who is moving. Include photos, phone numbers, and e-mail addresses.

- Provide your child with a picture of your new home.

- Keep schedules and routines as consistent as possible.

- For the move itself, be sure to bring along a favorite blanket and a few treasured items.

- When you arrive, set up the children's rooms first so that they feel safe and secure before you arrange the rest of your belongings.

- Visit the library, the YMCA, the park, and other available resources, so that your child begins to feel comfortable in your new place.

- If you move during the middle of a school year, arrange for your child to visit the school—before jumping in to attend every day.

Separation from a parent can be particularly difficult for a child. A young father shared, "My wife is deployed overseas, and my two-year-old is not sleeping. I know it's normal for a toddler to be fussy, but I worry that the separation from her mother will have a long-term effect."

When a parent is deployed or located in another geographical location, putting together a picture book showing Mom or Dad at work, writing letters, and talking by phone or Internet can make all the difference in helping your child stay connected. Having the absent parent send home recordings or digital video of him reading a book aloud can make a child feel closer. Praying together for the absent parent or saying a special poem or rhyme can become a routine that comforts. Talking about what the family will do together when the parent returns can help even a young child look forward to being reunited.

Daily conversations about an absent parent can help a child show and express feelings. "Momma would like this soup. When she comes home, let's make some for her." "Let's take a picture and we can send it to Mommy." "Daddy would laugh at this joke. Let's send it to him tonight by e-mail." "Your dad will be so proud of you. I can't wait for you to tell him." Connections during absences can be as meaningful as those in person.

Children are sensitive to the emotions of their family members. Family challenges, such as a parent's job loss, can affect a child. You can turn even a difficult situation into a learning opportunity and happy memory for your child. A concerned father said, "I wanted to teach my children, 'I am not my circumstances. They do not define me.' But when I lost my job, it was such a challenge, and I felt traumatized. I tried to keep my four- and seven-year-old from my stress and to focus on teaching them new skills. The upside was that I had more time to spend with them, so I started taking them to the park or library after school. We picked up a cook book for children. We made just simple things at first, like eggs in the hole and pancakes, but they really had fun. I found that teaching them a new skill—how to use the peeler, the egg chopper, and rolling pin—turned out to be the best time. When I went back to work, we tried to keep up our new focus on healthy food and cooking together."

According to the National Center for Children in Poverty, one in five families struggles to make ends meet. Be aware and reach out to encourage and support someone who needs it. If you are laid off, lose your job, or experience a prolonged financial hardship, it is a critical time to be sensitive to your child. While it is an incredible challenge, this is the time to keep routines steady and to put a healthy psychological boundary between the problem and the child.

If you choose to tell a child about the situation, share what happened in simple, age-appropriate terms. "Dad is looking for a new job." "We are going to stay with Grandma for a few weeks." As much as possible, make each day special with activities and conversations that are pleasant and positive. Reach out to community resources, and use the library, local parks, churches, and other organizations that provide activities for children.

It may be tempting to say, "Don't use too much soap . . . ," or "We don't have enough . . . ," but as much as possible, help the child focus on what you do have. "You can take a quick shower before we read extra stories." Keeping your child's focus on regular activities and minimizing worry is important.

In every difficult challenge and when the unexpected happens, you can be sure that your honesty, deep caring, and respect for your child's experience will make all the difference in the way she responds. Trust your intuition about what your child needs from you. Resilience is established over time and thrives when you are consistent and invested in your child's well-being. Your child's security is rooted in the strength of her relationship with you.

Welcoming a New Baby

When my son was born, my daughter was already five years old. With that large age gap, she was used to being the center of attention, and she was jealous. I scheduled some special dad-daughter time and took her out for breakfast. She really responded well to hearing us tell her that we couldn't raise the baby without her help.

When a baby brother or sister joins the family, children need reassurance. Help your older children understand what will happen when the baby arrives. Reading age-appropriate books or making your own picture book before the baby comes can help your children know what to expect. They may imagine that the baby will be able to play ball right away or might be shocked when the baby burps and cries and takes up Mommy's time.

With family-centered birthing centers and clinics that allow sibling visits, the transition to home can go smoothly. Meeting the baby before she arrives home can help siblings understand how tiny she is. When mom walks in the front door, someone else should hold baby, so mom's arms are open for a big hug.

Many parents want the older child to act like a big boy or girl and may worry when she wants to suck on a pacifier or roll up in a baby blanket. It may seem counterintuitive, but allowing your child to act like a baby for a while will help her tire of it more quickly. It is not that much fun to lie still when there are lots of exciting things to be explored. Double up on cuddle time, and let an older child stay near. There will be times when an older sibling wants to snuggle nearby when you are feeding the baby. If you let the older child curl up next to you, she will quickly move on, assured that you want her to be part of the new baby's relationship with you. This reassurance and inclusion will increase the bond of caring between siblings.

When older siblings are with the baby, continue to focus on what to do: "You are so gentle when you touch baby," instead of, "Don't poke." "It's so sweet to snuggle with you and the baby." Be sure to remind your older child how much she can do that the baby cannot do, such as going to the park with Grandma, building with her new tool set, and putting together a puzzle. Older children will appreciate your love and thanks when they help with their new baby brother or sister.

If you are the parent of multiples, be sure to join a support group and learn all you can about the unique challenges siblings experience when the new baby is actually two or more babies. The happier you are in adjusting to the babies, the more smoothly things will go for all of your children. Knowing what works for other parents can be reassuring.

Don't try to handle everything by yourself. One mom said, "When my twins were born, I had a responsible twelve-year-old come over to play with my two-year-old son on weeknights while I gave the babies a bath and put them to bed." Having an extra pair of hands during bath time or meal time, or to fold laundry with you can mean the difference between sanity and feeling overwhelmed.

Keep it simple: "Remember the rules." "Gentle hands." "Walking feet." Stating things simply helps children focus on what needs to be done—and keeps everyone calm.

If you have another caregiver, be sure to describe her responsibilities in detail. Your first thoughts will be to focus on the baby's needs, but be sure you go into detail about the older child or children. If an older child goes elsewhere during the day, plan a care bag with snacks, a special activity, and a love note from you tucked in.

There is much that can be done to encourage happy feelings for all. Give your children enough of you, and let them know that you love them as they are. Your open heart will show the siblings how much room is there for everyone. Here are some ideas to get started:

- **Infants and toddlers**

  ► Look at picture books together about what babies can do.

  ► Plan special times together so each child feels loved and secure.

  ► Give a new baby doll to a toddler sibling, and encourage role-playing baby-care routines.

  ► Encourage cuddling, hugging, and rocking with you.

- **Preschool-age children**

  ► Schedule major changes such as toilet training, a move to a big-kid bed, and new child-care arrangements before the new baby comes, or wait until things have settled into a regular routine.

  ► Involve your child in helping you shop for and arrange baby items.

  ► Have your child pack her own special bag to use when Mom goes to the hospital. Include a love note, pictures, a little gift, books, and special pajamas.

- ▸ Plan extra time with family, including grandparents or family friends.

- ▸ Take extra time to read, play games, and do special activities together. Make sure to plan fifteen minutes each day to focus on each child.

- **Elementary-age children**

  - ▸ Wait to tell a child that Mom is pregnant. Nine months is a long time to wait! When Mom is showing and the baby is kicking is a good time to share.

  - ▸ Teach about new babies using age-appropriate language, so that the children can understand the changes in Mom's body and have realistic expectations.

  - ▸ Let your child visit in the hospital.

  - ▸ Involve your child in baby-care routines, such as helping attach diapers or dispensing lotion.

  - ▸ Keep children's school and home routines consistent.

Your children will be together long after you are gone. Enjoy the precious moments you have with them, realizing that they will grow up so quickly. Keep enjoying the remarkable people they are becoming. And take lots of pictures.

Coping with Illness

> My husband was diagnosed with a kidney disease and needed dialysis. It was a really hard time for our three kids as their dad was in the hospital for over a month. When he finally got home, it was a long recovery. My children had to step up to look out for each other. We had many talks about chipping in to be extra caring and helpful.

Talking about how to handle illness is important. You may have been nurtured and comforted when you were sick, or you may be less comfortable with illness. One parent said, "My mother once told me, 'I can't handle your being sick when I need to work.' I know she meant well, but instead of just feeling bad from my 101-degree fever, I also felt bad about getting sick." When you are faced with an ill family member, your most nurturing self or your true discomfort will show. Be realistic and honest about what you can handle and what support you need. Compassionate resources are available to assist with the difficult challenges of caring for a chronically ill child or family member and to help you find your way through emotional stress and uncertainty. This is a time to accept the love and support of others who can cover practical needs while you focus on meeting the needs of your family.

Children who have been sick for a prolonged period of time or who are hospitalized often become very tuned into others and want to make the most of every day. They are sensitive to their parents' emotions and will rely on their optimism and encouragement. Children need their parents to be honest and to use words and ideas that they can understand. If your child has a chronic illness, it is important to focus on what you can do to make each day special.

It can help to put a "comfort box" together with items to lift the spirits of the sick person. For a sick child, a book, a stuffed animal, some fresh colored pencils and paper, and a game to play together tucked into a basket with a card really can make a difference. "I am cheering for you," is the needed message. Daily spirit lifters are essential. Many siblings of sick children feel left out and often feel guilty about their feelings. Because the focus and balance of the entire family shifts, they want and need to know that you treasure your time with them.

At the end of the day, remind your children that they are special and loved. Help them look for something good, both about the day that is finished and the one that lies ahead.

When a parent is ill, the other parent or caregivers will need to take time to set aside medical issues and focus on the children and their needs. Everyone needs to keep schedules and supports as normal as possible and to set aside time to really connect.

There are many books for children to help them talk about their feelings and experiences. National, state, and local organizations can provide information and support for specific illnesses and help families during this time.

- The American Cancer Society provides information on helping children when they or a family member is sick: http://www.cancer.org/treatment/childrenandcancer/index

- The American Psychological Association gives practical help for supporting children and family members during chronic illness: http://www.apa.org/helpcenter/chronic -illness-child.aspx

- The National Academy of Pediatrics provides information on helping children cope with sickness, disasters, and grief: http://www.aap.org/en-us/advocacy-and-policy /aap-health-initiatives/Children-and-Disasters/Pages/Promoting-Adjustment-and -Helping-Children-Cope.aspx

Be sure to spend time alone with each child in your family, focusing on the good things that have happened. Let each child know how much she is cherished, and give her something to hold on to—hope, enthusiasm, and eagerness about the day that follows. Express your love and gratitude for each day, and tell your children how much joy they bring to you.

Experiencing Grief and Loss

When our cat died, we told our three young children, 'Smokey was hurting so much and couldn't get better.' They watched their daddy bury him and place a stone over his grave. The children held a funeral for him. They still like going to visit his gravestone and talking about him.

Pets provide a significant bond of love for young children. Losing a beloved pet can feel almost like the loss of a family member. If children have witnessed the death, such as seeing a pet being run over by a car, they will be visibly upset and may be inconsolable at the time. Stay sensitive to their questions, and take your cues from the child. Don't be surprised if for some time the child seems okay, and then weeks later, she revisits the sadness. Letting children grieve fully can help them move on to the next step of honoring and remembering their pet.

For children who have already lost a parent or other loved one, the loss of a beloved pet can reawaken the original grief. A dad said, "When I was ten and my dog died, I was devastated and cried for weeks. I didn't realize until I was much older that the loss of my Lab had given me the opportunity to grieve the earlier loss of my mother. I am sensitive now to how attached my children are to our dog and cat."

Many children will want to have a funeral service for the pet. This is an appropriate way for them to share and talk about their memories. Younger children can draw pictures and will appreciate a photo book. A stuffed animal—such as a bunny if a bunny has passed away—can be consoling, and children will cuddle it at night as a way of comforting themselves.

Try to keep your child focused on happy activities and events. Arrange a sleepover, a craft event, or a day trip with a best friend. It is important for children to know that things are going to be okay and that you are helping them move forward with confidence and keeping their life on track.

> *When my mom got sick, we had to be gentle, so the children learned to be caring and gentle. We would say, "Grandma's hand isn't working." We took one step at a time. It was scary for Bailey to see someone who used to be active but now was in a wheelchair and couldn't respond. We told Lucas when Grandma got a breathing mask that it was like an astronaut uniform that would help her breathe.*

> *When she went into a coma, we talked about our faith and how Grandma was going to heaven where it is really beautiful, and she will see Jesus and the angels and won't be sick anymore. One evening at home, when we told them that Grandma had passed away, they both cheered—actually jumped up and down. We asked why they were cheering, and Bailey said, "Because Grandma is in heaven."*

> *We thought the funeral would be too overwhelming for them, with adults crying. But after the burial, the children wanted to go and put flowers around her grave. They did it in their own time and way, in private. Afterward, we talked about how Grandma was still a part of them and always loved them. We keep her memory close to us by reminding them of the places we went with her and wonderful times we had.*

When a parent or someone who has been close to your family dies, it is important to trust your knowledge of each child and to let her lead the way. Even if a death is sudden, you can still take the time children need. Answer a little at a time, in a way that matches their understanding. If you have a faith tradition, those beliefs and practices can guide your conversation. Children can be resilient when they know that what is around them is secure.

When children do raise questions, it's important to answer them honestly, but only as much as a child wants to know. Children may want to know who will take care of them, get them ready for school, or put them to bed. They may be afraid that something will happen to you. Take each day step by step, answering with only what the child can handle and keeping routines as consistent as possible.

Children usually take their cues from adults to see how upset they are. Let your children know that feelings are good and need to be expressed. A child can be told, "It's okay to cry and to feel sad." Of course, your children may see you cry, but you want to save your deepest tears, fears, and struggles to share with friends and other adults. Protect a space of security for your children.

Help children put together a collage of pictures or display photo books of their loved one to help them talk about their feelings. Books for children about death can help open the conversation. (See page 191 for recommended children's books.) Let them know it's okay to talk about their feelings any time they want to and that you are there for them.

Young children will need extra support at bedtime and additional focused time in the weeks and months that follow. They can decorate a box and place inside special items that remind them of their parent or loved one, such as pictures, gifts, or mementos. Making up a poem about the person who has died and placing it with a picture under the child's pillow for sweet dreams can bring comfort. Help younger children design a special pillow with marker or fabric paint that has pictures and words about the person they miss. Ask friends of the family to write a memory book that tells special stories and memories about the person who has died, so that the child can keep this treasured gift.

Accept the comfort level a child desires. One parent made a quilt for her son out of t-shirts his dad used to wear. A little girl often wore her mother's pajamas to bed after her mom died, as this felt comforting to her. Even if it seems silly to you, support the child's choices and needs. Make sure to talk often about what the person loved, remembering certain foods, places, and activities you shared. Most of all, talk often about the person's love for your child. All of these will help your child stay connected to the love she feels for this special person.

Thriving after Divorce

Our children were afraid that I was going to leave them because their dad had left. We did our best to reassure them constantly.

Divorce can throw your life for a loop. The immediate issues can complicate your thinking, and daily decisions must be made within new frameworks of security. The challenge is to balance your emotional equilibrium while figuring out new ways to live.

The key to finding an emotional center of strength in the midst of change is to make conscious decisions that are healthy and in your best interest. Stick with "what you know for sure," and trust yourself. You don't have to figure out everything at once. However, there are some reliable approaches that can make things easier:

- **Be your best self.** If you need motivation, remember that the messages you teach are anchored in how you live each day. Start by vowing to take care of yourself physically, emotionally, and spiritually. Children will rebound more quickly when they see that you are going to be okay. This is what they want more than anything else—to know that you will be strong and there for them. Your children will take their cues from you—who you are today. So take yourself and your health seriously.

- **Get counseling to deal with hurts.** Now is the time to set healthy boundaries. Children do not need to know about all the issues you are facing. They are in the middle of their own world and need you to keep a strong buffer between your journey and their lives. Seek a trusted counselor who can help you talk things out and sort out the issues while you make decisions.

- **Keep routines predictable.** Set the table. Put out flowers. Bring balloons for special occasions. Keep the schedule. Honor family traditions and celebrations.

- **Plan activities that the children enjoy.** Focus on fun and learning rather than on buying and entertainment. While an occasional movie, sporting event, or festival can be fun, aim for time together at the park, a lake, the zoo, the library, or even the grocery store. Celebrate daily life.

- **Keep conversation open and set aside time for each child.** Ask open-ended questions. Really listen. Connect and express your care and reassurance. Remind them often, "It's not your fault." "I love you and always will." "I will be there for you."

- **Be clear about expectations with your ex—and be responsible in keeping your part.** When exchanging your children, stick to the subject. Say something positive about the children: "Mary had a good day in math today. She can tell you about it." "Have a good time. I will see you tomorrow at 3:00."

- **Monitor inner self-talk and keep it positive.** Switch, "I don't know how I can handle this," to "It's a hard day today, but I am going to do this one step at a time," or "Even though this decision is difficult, I am going to take a break and focus on something else." You don't have to deny what is difficult, but be sure to set the current issue within the context of determination and hope. The goal is to get stronger, make good decisions, and create a good life for yourself and your children.

- **When you face a hard day, turn toward positive and healthy forms of comfort.** Don't isolate yourself or rely on unhealthy responses to stress, such as eating unhealthy foods, giving in to anger, shifting into negative thinking, spending money you don't have, or drinking or self-medicating. Reach out to a support network of friends. Plan to get out, and keep your focus. Start a new workout routine, read a new book, or begin a project. Listen to happy music, and keep up your own predictable schedule.

- **Watch your words.** If you can't say something positive, don't say anything at all. Remember that life moves in the directions of our thoughts. The messages you internalize and send become your reality. You set the emotional thermostat for your children, so be purposeful about making positive conversation. Ask specific questions. "Tell me about art class. What colors did you paint the sculpture you made on Tuesday?" "What games did you play at recess?" Share happy times about your own day: "The best part of my day was when the delivery truck came and I watched him unload the wood for the neighbor. What was the best part of your day?" Don't miss the extraordinary in the ordinary.

- **Ask for help when you need it.** Ask specifically for what you need. Don't wait until you are coming unglued. Try to anticipate when you could use help—someone to run errands or keep you company.

- **Be patient.** Don't try to fix everything at once. If relatives or friends want to talk and you aren't ready, simply say, "Thank you for caring. I don't feel I can talk about it yet."

- **Trust your relationships.** People who really love you are going to stick by you. Be patient with yourself, as well as others.

It may be instinctive to want to belittle the other parent or try to get children on your side. This is sure to backfire. Children need you to be a stable home base and will only resent or feel upset that you are raising conflicts regarding things for which they are not responsible. No matter what happened, there is only one direction to take that can lead you to a solid future. Choose to take a path toward health, wellness, and security for you and your children.

Divorce moves families into new life territory. Find the ways that work best for your children. Count on good things ahead. Revitalize your focus, and know that you are modeling to your children what a healthy person does during difficult times of change. Life will go on. It will not be the same. It will be different—and it will be good.

> Make up a story that illustrates the same feelings your child is experiencing. Ask your child what the other child (or character) should do. Seeing the situation from a new perspective can give your child the opportunity to gain new insights.

Reflecting on the Journey

I heard the Dr. Seuss quote, "Don't cry because it's over. Smile because it happened." I didn't realize how much I would think about my own childhood when I had kids.

It may be that in learning about how you want to raise your children, you find areas of your own life and experience that need healing. This may mean identifying and responding to your own disappointments or unfinished grief or memories. When you have a child, you have the opportunity to become children again in the best sense and to fulfill the journey of your own life story. As you view the world through your child's eyes, be reminded of how you felt as a child, and remember what nourished you and gave you a sense of wholeness.

Inspire your children to live up to their fullest potential. To parent with freedom, you must first enter your own journey of discovery and maximize the power of resilience in your own life. It is in understanding yourself that you will come to understand the lives of your children. By exploring your pathway, you can parent more wisely.

Whether stresses are few and far between or you are facing significant challenges, you can build your children's strengths and increase the protective factors that will help them have a healthy future. The goal is to build the resources of strength and flexibility that can help them withstand life's setbacks.

When you face times of uncertainty, it can undermine your sense of security. How long will this situation go on? Is there hope for a positive outcome? It is instinctive to wait until you know an outcome before you reorient and make a positive plan of action. However, the choices you make about your self-care and mental health are essential to your recovery. Take confident steps forward that will influence your children in the way they adapt.

Many of us were taught that if we just did the right things, that life would turn out right. But even with the best of intentions, difficult challenges come. When you have others behind you to encourage you, you will have support and will reorient your vision when the way is dark. This positive outlook is what you need to teach your children. They will need to regroup when they don't do well in school, make peace when they disagree with friends, and pick themselves up when things go wrong.

Much of what children learn will be the unspoken lessons that you model to them. In the end, it will be the way you live, rather than what you tell them, that will have the greatest influence. The important goal is to reframe failure and disappointment as an opportunity to learn and grow. Help your children rebound by fostering empathy for self and others, and help them to see growth itself as a lifelong process.

All children need love, nurturing, consistency, and support to develop resilience. Focusing on strengths, building assets, and treating each child with love and respect will make all the difference. In the midst of trying times, children's capacity to love and be loved is ever present. Your nurturing and caring guidance can help them blossom into all they are meant to be.

CHAPTER 7
TURNING AROUND CHALLENGING BEHAVIOR

Identifying Solutions when Your Buttons Are Pushed

My son used to throw temper tantrums when he was tired. I taught him to bring his favorite stuffed animal to me. Before he would melt down, I would say, "Do you want some Teddy time?" Then he would go and get Teddy—before he got upset.

All parents have moments when our children's behavior feels challenging and we are nearing our wits' end. What are the "button-pusher behaviors" that bother you? For many people, they include whining, sibling rivalry, being wild, talking back, eyeball rolling, making faces, and not coming when called. Most of the time, the behavior involves "just not doing what I want them to do."

Take, for example, eye rolling. One mom said, "I just tell my daughter, 'I can see you still have something you want to say. Your face tells me as much as your words.' That strategy always works for me, because she usually does have more to say." Another mom laughed, "I just tell my daughter, 'You just roll those eyeballs back around the other way, sister!' That usually defuses the situation with humor and we end up with a hug." If parents ignore a behavior completely, it probably would not become an issue. But each of these moms has chosen to engage in a discussion about their daughters' eye rolling. The trick is to make your button-pushing experience conscious, so that you can act rather than react, and keep yourself out of a cycle of frustration. Knowing your triggers can help you be more effective in responding.

One dad asked, "Why do I get so angry when my child fiddles with his shoelaces when I am talking to him?" Another dad responded, "Someone must have gotten mad at you for the same thing when you were a child." The first dad replied, "Come to think of it, I did have a babysitter who got so mad at me that she tied my shoelaces together. Maybe I am still upset over that!" He laughed, but amazingly, the shoelace issue didn't bother him so much anymore.

The urge to yell back when your child yells or become angry when your child is angry can be interrupted not merely by a technique such as breathing deeply or talking quietly on purpose, but also by seeing your child through the lens of empathy. Often, validation and a hug or a box of tissues can defuse a situation. When your child knows you will stay calm, his own anger or upset can de-escalate, as well.

> Focus on the goal. Don't take behavior personally. Instead, look for positive ways to turn the situation around.

Some parents may say, "I am so frustrated," or "That makes me angry," after they describe a behavior. Of course it is okay at times to share how you feel, but you don't want young children to stop doing something because someone else is angry or frustrated with them. You don't want them to comply to try to fix a parent's feelings. Instead, you want them to become caring and self-directed.

Tell your child when something really matters to you: "When I am making dinner, I really need your help. What can you do to keep yourselves happy until I am ready?" Your child may say, "I want to help you." He may say, "I will go play." Simply describe the situation without emotion, so that the child can focus on positive options.

You want children to tune in and notice what is going around them and to respond thoughtfully. "It would be helpful for you and Karla to find something else to do. Do you have school work, or do you want to play?" A choice or incompatible alternative helps children refocus their attention. You might ask, "How can we make this work better?" You may be surprised by what they tell you. Most children want to be part of the solution.

Following are questions to help you identify strategies when there are frustrations or meltdowns.

- Have you let the behavior go on after the first time or have you responded inconsistently?

- Did you miss teaching a needed skill?

- Have you inadvertently tried to stop—rather than replace—the misbehavior?

- Have you rewarded the misbehavior by giving attention to it?

- Did you prepare the child ahead of time for what was expected?

- Did you give enough support so that the child followed through successfully?

- Did you inadvertently set up a power struggle?

- Is the child ill, tired, or hungry?

- Are you under stress, ill, exhausted, or hungry?

- Did you ask the child for input?

- What is the child's tone of voice telling you? What is his body language showing you? Is he reaching his limit?

Tuning in to your child's cues can help you turn an entire morning around. Stepping in early can save the day. Help your older children to notice and respond to their own needs sooner, before they become upset or distressed. Make the situation as easy on yourself—and on them—as you can.

Focusing on the best way to move everyone forward can keep you from overreacting to button-pushing moments. You can ask, "How can I make this situation turn out well? What can I say or do now to keep us focused on our goal?" Keep things in perspective and hold in mind the thing that matters most—your relationship with your child.

Negotiating Meltdowns with Confidence

My daughter threw up her breakfast while having a tantrum. I wanted to flip out, but I stayed calm and put her in a safe place on a towel, cleaned up the vomit very calmly, and said, "When you are finished crying, then

you can come and play puzzles. If you need a hug, I can give you a hug."
It was the hardest thing I ever did, but after about four minutes, she
stopped crying and came over and crawled into my lap.

The truth is that when a child is having a screaming fit or tantrum, the person who needs calming is the parent or caregiver. No child will cry forever, so staying cool, calm, and collected during the upset is the first requirement. According to researchers James Green, Pamela Whitney, and Michael Potegal, a tantrum progresses in a normal and expected sequence of events. If you intervene too soon, it only makes matters worse. The most effective response from parents is to do nothing while waiting for the upset to subside. This is very difficult for most adults to do. For infants, always respond to crying with soothing. For toddlers and preschoolers, be sure the child is in a safe place, and wait for the tantrum to finish.

Attempts at intervention by parents, such as pleading to stop, threats, promises, and more can make the situation worse. If you cave in and buy the child something, tempt him with something from your purse, or give in to a request, your response will increase the likelihood of the child having a tantrum again. In public places, children may cry, whine, or have a tantrum because they are legitimately tired or stressed. On the other hand, if their behavior has been reinforced and rewarded before, you have set up a power struggle and patterns that will take effort to break. You have inadvertently taught that good behavior can be bargained for.

It is always helpful to tune in to frustrations and intervene early. Often you can step in ahead of time and say, "Oh, I can see that's hard. Do you need help?" This can go a long way to help your child express frustrations without acting them out. Pay attention to what happens to trigger a child's upset feelings. The next time the child is in the same situation, you will know to step in early.

Keep your eyes and mind on what is happening. Don't wait until the child is hungry, tired, distressed, or out of control to step in.

A child is not capable of turning a behavior pattern around. He cannot analyze the steps, figure out what is not working, and change it. He is still gaining emotional understanding and the ability to calm and soothe himself. Changing the child's behavior is the role and responsibility of the adult. Children need an adult to help them talk out—instead of act out—their frustrations.

Calming a Child Who Is out of Control

My son gets so wound up, and his energy drives me crazy. There are times I want to yell, but getting upset only makes it worse. I take him by the hand and send him outside. I want him to know that I will step in when he can't help or stop himself.

When a child is out of control or becoming out of control, he needs to know that you will step in immediately to stop behaviors that are dangerous or destructive. Children really don't want to be out of control. They feel upset, anxious, angry, agitated, and distressed. They want to know that adults are there to give needed boundaries for their emotions and behaviors.

A regular calming space at home or a quiet place when you are out will work for a break until a child is ready to come back and behave more productively. The child is in control here. He can determine how long he needs to reflect, refocus, or calm down. He can decide when he is ready to rejoin an activity or try again. Some children enjoy calming bottles—plastic bottles filled with colored water, mineral oil, and glitter. They can tilt a calming bottle back and forth, making the contents roll around. Other children like to curl up with a stress ball or stuffed animal. A break is a way for children to calm themselves, breathe deeply, and rejoin the activity when they are ready.

When your child's behavior escalates, you can ask him to step out of the action for a few minutes to take a break. Stay firm: "When you get yourself together, then you may come back." This lets your child know that you will not let misbehavior continue. It also shows that you are putting him in charge of his own behavior. "When you have a plan in your head for what to do next, I can help you get started."

Younger children may want and need assistance. "Do you want me to take a few minutes with you, or do you want to take some time alone?" Often children want to be comforted and will respond well. Be sure to say, "Next time, come get a hug before you get upset or before you need help finding something to do."

> Encourage your child to take some time to calm down, think more clearly, and keep from reacting in a negative way, or to chill out for a few minutes alone or with you.

Of course, it is better to anticipate and step in before a child falls apart or becomes angry. Being proactive is the best plan of action. "Layla, please take a break so you can calm down and make a better choice. You can come back when you have taken a few deep breaths and can pay attention to what your body is doing." Children want and need strategies that work.

Eventually children will learn to take a break before they get into a frustration or scuffle. They will learn to recognize when they feel out of control. And children learn that breaks are for everyone. Give yourself a break to allow a stressful situation to defuse, which will help you feel better and will give the people you love a chance to take a break as well.

Use a taking a break as part of a calming and thinking plan, not as shame or punishment. If you use this option respectfully, children will respond well, realizing you are giving them a chance to come back and make a better choice. This approach is very different from a traditional time-out, which sets up a power struggle. A time-out is the adult's way of saying, "Do this, or I will make you." Assigning a child a number of minutes in a corner or on a chair only stops a behavior for a moment and has a number of negative side effects. According to parenting expert Peter Haiman and child-development expert Kirsten Haugen, time-outs may increase resentment and cause children to hide behaviors instead of willfully engaging in cooperation. The child complies to avoid punishment, but the behavior usually returns. Instead, focus your child's attention on cooperation, helpfulness, and self-discipline. The unwanted behavior is less likely to return because the child has self-regulated.

Once a child gets used to taking a break, he will begin to use this technique on his own. Many children will walk away from a sibling and go to their room just as the anger bubbles up and before they act out. When you see your child make this choice, notice and comment on the behavior. It is a sign of growing maturity.

Using the Environment Wisely

Having my second child has really taught me to be more patient and understanding. I realize that, when a baby comes, everyone is adjusting. I am the one who has to be careful about limits and needs to be ready to help my three-year-old move on when she is disappointed or upset.

A change of physical space can work wonders when children are cranky or out of sorts. Giving each child a box to climb in, along with a flashlight and book, can provide needed time apart. Building a fort by covering two chairs with a blanket can provide private space to play quietly.

A mother of a baby and a two-year-old said, "When the baby is napping, I let my toddler play in the bathtub with the bath toys—without any water! He just loves going in there and making his animals "talk" and lining up the cars on the side of the tub. It's kind of funny to see him there fully clothed, but I get a few minutes to go to the bathroom, check my e-mails, and read my morning devotional book."

If an infant or toddler is fussy, going outside for a walk or taking an indoor walk can shift the mood. A few minutes in the bathroom making funny faces together in the mirror can help you both feel better. Bringing a basket of toys to another room can reorient attention. Changing places can restore a child's focus, alleviate monotony, and help you keep your perspective.

If you can send your children safely outside to jump, run, and swing, take advantage of the change in setting. If you and your child need a break, but you must be with your children at all times when they are outdoors, make wise use of your indoor environment. Here are some strategies to try:

> If the child's misbehavior cannot be redirected, move to another room or location. Go outside.

- **Make space.** Push back your furniture to make a dancing area in the middle of a room. Move the kitchen table to create space for indoor ice skating. Stay close to supervise, and let the child wear socks as they "skate" around.

- **Use tape.** Create a large painter's-tape square on the floor for rolling, dancing, or gymnastics. You can tape off a "running course." Children can run back and forth to touch the opposite walls.

- **Create big-body games.** Tape off an indoor hopscotch grid. Use bean bags for tossing.

- **Modify activities.** Try indoor jump rope, in which the rope swings back and forth near the floor instead of swinging around over the head of the child. Secure one end of the rope to a table leg.

- **Be creative.** Provide a rope or tape on the floor for the child to use as a tightrope. He can walk forward and backward and can balance in different poses.

- **Get active.** Make an indoor obstacle course with boxes to climb through, pillows to climb over, and a sheet to roll across.

- **Play sports.** Encourage indoor sports such as basketball and bowling. For basketball, toss balled-up socks into a laundry basket. Different sock colors can earn different point values. For bowling, use closed, partially filled water bottles as pins, and use the balled-up socks or tennis balls as bowling balls.

- **Get wet.** Set up supervised water play in a dishpan. Use measuring cups, plastic tubes, and containers. Place the tub on a tabletop or on the floor on top of an old shower curtain. Alternately, let the children put on bathing suits and go "swimming" in the bathtub.

- **Play restaurant.** Place a cloth on top of a box. Your children can make a menu and draw pictures of the food. Older children can decide how much each item will cost. Giving real or pretend money to spend can make this a fun learning activity.

- **Play vet's office.** Help the children set up a veterinarian's office using items from around your home. Add some ripped rags to use as bandages and a white shirt for a doctor's coat. Pretend to help sick or wounded stuffed animals.

- **Play bakery.** Use simple household items, such as baskets and kitchen tools and pans, and encourage the children to create yummy pretend baked goods to sell.

- **Explore with household items.** Toddlers love to fill empty plastic bottles with pom-poms or fit pipe-cleaner pieces into empty spice bottles. A plastic bag of paper-towel tubes, empty yogurt containers, or paper cups can be balanced and stacked as part of a "circus" act. Creativity is inexpensive.

- **Go shopping.** Before a trip to the store, let your children use clipboards, paper, and pencils to make shopping lists. They can cut pictures of items needed from a newspaper or magazine and glue these onto the lists. When you go shopping, the children can check items off their lists. This will engage them in meaningful activity that takes their mind off of boredom or frustration.

There is no magic way to change children's behavior. Most misbehavior stems from children's boredom, overstimulation, or need for a change of pace. Rather than focusing on the unwanted behavior, move the children to another area of the house and get them engaged in doing something positive with their energy and imaginations. Busy hands and minds are less likely to find other outlets for their energy.

Redirecting and Repurposing Energy

The boys have constant energy. As crazy as it seems, we got a puppy. The boys now go outside in the morning and run around with him. They ride their bikes while I run the dog. Playing with the puppy helps them all get along better and get their energy out.

It's okay for children to have high energy. The challenge for parents is redirecting and repurposing that energy. Challenges are opportunities for you to be creative in your thinking.

According to the Institute of Medicine, as well as researchers Russell Pate et al., children need to move and enjoy active play two to three hours a day for adequate sensory involvement, balance experience, and tactile stimulation. This includes at least fifteen minutes of active play per hour. Exercise lowers stress and anxiety and reduces aggression. Side benefits of active play include healthier weight and the ability to focus more when learning.

Get and stay active with your children by taking walks, dancing, or riding bikes together. Give enough outdoor time for free play that includes jumping, running, and climbing. Building aerobic activity into each day's schedule helps children feel calmer.

Be realistic in your expectations when you ask your children to sit still. One mom said that, after she and her son exited an office building in the city, the boy threw his arms wildly in the air, spun around, and jumped. A young woman from a group nearby smiled and said, "I'll bet your boy sat a long time waiting for you and that you really appreciated it!" The child had been cooped up so long that he could hardly contain himself. Asking a child to wait at a meeting or sit a

> Don't let a dangerous behavior continue, hoping that it will go away. Step in and move your child to another place right away. Children need to know that you will intervene.

long time at a restaurant intended for adults is not in anyone's best interest. Be fair to your children, to yourself, and to others.

When your children are wound up and getting out of control, they need your assistance. Intervene before the noise level rises, the protesting begins in earnest, or the activity level puts children at risk of getting hurt. Stepping in immediately—before things get out of hand—is the best plan. You will have avoided getting angry and the children will still be in a frame of mind to respond. If you walk in on a situation that has escalated, take steps to help reorient the energy and focus.

Taking the Sizzle out of Sibling Rivalry

Sometimes they get along like angels, and other times, they are so mean. I just want the girls to get along, and I want them to enjoy their time together.

For better or worse, siblings have an enormous impact on each other's lives. Siblings can buffer stress, help each other learn to negotiate and compromise, and boost language and social skills. The downside is that difficult sibling relationships can become a negative influence—one that may be hard to resolve.

Like every aspect of parenting, become aware of your own contribution and understand your ability to turn things around. If your own relationship with a sibling was challenging, you may inadvertently accept sibling aggression as normal. In that case, be aware of how your own experiences can shape your perspective, and focus on nurturing cooperation instead of conflict between your children. When one sibling struggles with another, avoid excusing unkindness by saying, "Oh, she didn't mean it." or "Sorry. She is tired." Making excuses for thoughtless behavior invites similar behavior in the future and encourages retaliation. The habit of excusing behavior is a pattern that can be quickly picked up by the children themselves. Instead, say, "I am sorry she wasn't able to control her actions and use her words. I know that hurt your feelings. I am sorry that happened." Then, you can revisit the issue with both children by talking about what happened and brainstorming solutions.

It is better not to make a child apologize, as he may continue the unkind behavior, knowing it can be excused afterward. Or, a child may say he is sorry but not really feel sorry. By forcing an apology, you may cause him to say something that is not true. Over time, your example of apologizing for the child will be picked up, and he will begin to do it by himself.

Reading children's books about getting along with siblings can help children appreciate and understand the special love that is in their family. (See the list of recommended children's books on page 191.) Following are additional tips that can increase sibling empathy and cooperation, especially as children grow older:

- **Reserve private spaces.** Beds belong to the person who sleeps in them. Before one child climbs into another's bed or enters another's space, he should ask permission. Be sure every child has a space for things that are theirs alone. Honoring boundaries will minimize jealousy.

- **Keep toys and books separate.** Some items can be shared by agreement. Others should be the property of the child to whom they belong. A basket of special books and items can be kept privately next to the child's bed.

- **Honor the birthday child.** Gifts are for the child who is being celebrated. Talk with your other child or children ahead of time about what to expect at a family celebration. Ask the other child to be the paper crusher, bow gatherer, or helper.

- **Teach active listening skills.** "Micah, let's all look and listen to Isabel now. I will focus on you next." "We listen to what someone has to say before we answer." Teach skills for good conversation, such as taking turns, nodding when someone talks, and asking questions to learn more. "What else did you do?" "Where did you go next?"

- **Monitor communication.** Let each child speak for himself. Don't ask one child what another child did or said. Don't talk about a child in front of another child. Keep conversations between you and a child confidential. Keep report card and school information private, as well.

- **Encourage fun.** Organize projects for siblings to do together that are fun for both. Cooking, games, mini-cleaning projects, and organizing a small area can build teamwork.

- **Support skill independence.** Competent children feel good about themselves. Teach children to crack an egg, pour milk, or replace a toilet-paper roll.

- **Encourage cooperation instead of competition.** Be careful not to compare children verbally and to encourage shared cooperation toward a goal. For example, say, "When you both get your clothes on, we will head to the park," instead of, "See who can get their clothes on the fastest."

- **Know when to step in.** All children need to know that an adult is present to step in and protect their safety. When one child is hurting another child physically, it is critical that a parent steps in immediately to stop it: "I understand that you are angry, but I cannot let you hurt your brother. You can be angry, but you cannot hurt someone else. Let's cool off and take a break before you come back to play." Even if one child has instigated or upset the other child, intervention is important. Say, "It is my job to ensure that you both are safe. I will not allow either of you to hurt each other physically or with words." Teach children to walk away and get help when they are being hurt. Do not let patterns of teasing or bullying persist.

Give each child focused time alone with you to help him feel secure in your love and care. Children who feel that they have enough of you are much less likely to compete for your attention. Tuck away the electronics, and take time to make each child the center of your world. The way you treat your children will affect the way they treat each other. You are teaching them how to be best friends for life.

Knowing What to Do about Biting and Hitting

When I returned to work after my youngest was born, I found that when I came home in the afternoon, my nineteen-month-old would hit me. I felt bad that he was mad at me. Of course I knew he was upset and anxious about all the changes to his routine. I took his hands in mine and said, "I know you are upset. I can't let you hurt me. Do you need a hug?" He started to cry. I knew he just couldn't tell me what he felt.

Toddlers do not always have the language to say what they need. This gap in language can be frustrating to them and to others. Because they are still developing the use of words, toddlers may hit or bite when they are angry or when they can't get what they need or want. They may bite when they are bored and don't have enough challenge or when they are frustrated by something that is too complicated.

Biting and hitting happens most often during transitions or when a toddler is under stress or lacks a consistent routine. In a group setting, toddlers will become frustrated if they have not interacted with an adult in the past few minutes. They may hit in self-defense or in imitation of others. Knowing this, you can intervene beforehand and develop strategies to keep it from happening in the first place. The following strategies work to reduce frustration in toddlers:

- **Stay aware.** Anticipate children's needs, and be ready to step in. Encourage interaction with toys and games by modeling and staying nearby to facilitate play.

- **Minimize frustration.** Make sure there is enough space, access to materials, and adequate supplies and toys when multiple children are present. Set toys out in baskets for easy access.

- **Meet sensory needs.** To prevent biting related to sensory needs, offer your toddler foods with a range of textures, and provide appropriate objects on which to chew. Keep a container of pacifiers, teething rings, and other bitable objects that you can offer throughout the day.

- **Narrate what you see.** When an infant or toddler is looking around or reaching for something, talk about what he wants. "Oh, you want your truck. Can you see the truck next to the couch?"

- **Give alternatives.** Teach children what to do instead of biting or hitting. Teach simple words or cues that they can use to communicate when they need help. When they feel like biting, offer a teething ring or other object that is appropriate.

- **Make sure children have enough space and exercise.** Big body play, such as kicking balls, running, climbing, and rolling, is important to meet sensory and exercise needs. Children who are active are less likely to experience frustration from confinement and boredom.

Biting can be emotionally upsetting to a parent. But a toddler can't say, "I missed you today and am mad at you for leaving me," or "I'm frustrated that I can't play with the puzzle," so he shows his feelings through his actions. So be sure to put everything aside and join in his world. Anticipate his needs, and intervene before biting happens by giving him something to bite on. Then say, "It's okay. Mommy is here. Let's read a book together."

It is critical to evaluate how you respond after biting or hitting occurs. Refrain from an intense reaction and stay calm. Say quietly, "Biting hurts. We don't bite people. We use our mouths to blow kisses." Demonstrate blowing a kiss. Or say, "If you want to bite, you may bite a teething ring," or "Hitting hurts. Let's be gentle with our hands." Show the child how to stroke gently. Remain calm and teach other ways to communicate, such as simple words or signs.

When playing near others and in a group setting, monitor children constantly. Biting presents an opportunity to work together with others to support children's needs. This situation requires sensitivity and respect, realizing that you are teaching children to communicate and to care about others.

Solving Personal-Care Issues

> *It doesn't matter whether our daughter goes to bed on time or not; she gets up early and wakes up her brother. We want them to share a room together before the baby comes. What should we do?*

As children approach the preschool years, it is important to trust what is best for you and for your family. What you choose must match your child's unique temperament and must fit with your philosophy and lifestyle. Being consistent about your approach matters when it comes to sleeping through the night, staying in bed in the morning, potty training, and mealtimes.

Some parents don't mind when children come to cuddle with them in the morning. Others want them to stay in bed. The decision will be unique to each family. Following are some approaches parents have shared that worked well for them.

- We let our four-year-old crawl in bed with us in the morning. She snuggles and is really quiet. Sometimes she falls asleep. We love this time with her.

- We got a bunny clock that shows one bunny awake and another one sleeping. We say, "You can't wake up until both bunnies are awake." We set the clock timer that controls the bunny.

- We got a clock that turns color so George knows when to get up. This clock plays recorded stories, so he can lie quietly and listen. This story clock saved us.

- We gave Rose a special morning sleeping bear to snuggle with until the sun comes up.

- My four-year-old would wake up before 6:30 a.m. We made a morning bag with a granola bar, raisins, a few books, crayons, and toys and left it by his bed. We asked him to eat snacks and play in his room but not to wake us up until 7:00 a.m. We had a sticker chart and when he made it five days without waking us up, he got a treat. This all worked great.

- When our son got up at 5:00 a.m., we put him back to bed every single time. We gave him a few books and were firm: "We don't get up until it's get up time to get up." Because we were consistent, after three days it worked.

- We tried putting her to bed thirty to forty minutes later at night. This helped a lot. When she woke up early, we put her back in bed. We love to be with her, but we make sure she knows that sleep time is sleep time.

Teaching a young child to use a potty can be a real challenge. A mother with a new baby on the way was anxious to potty train her older child. She asked, "Do I have to stay home for a whole weekend and make my daughter drink constantly until she learns to go potty? What should we do?" Following is advice from parents of two- and three-year-olds who have successfully trained their children:

- Get lots of books on going to the potty. Let your child go at the same time as the same-sex parent. Make a big deal out of how big your child is and how much you love having a big kid.

- Make it fun. Always be positive and never punitive. Clean up accidents quietly and respectfully.

- We waited until he was ready and wanted to do it. We used a sticker chart and rewards, hung balloons in the bathroom, and played potty songs. He loved it, and we just made it into a big game.

- We put a potty chair on the floor, both downstairs and upstairs. He didn't like the big toilet seat or toilet cover. He didn't want to use the big potty until he was three and a half.

- My daughter loved to do it, and it passed by effortlessly. My son wore pull-up disposables at night until he was almost six. We never made an issue of it because he was a sound sleeper. I figured as long as he was okay during the day, it was okay at night. Our pediatrician said this was alright, too.

- I let my mother teach him. He loved learning to go potty at Grandma's one weekend, and they had a blast. He came home to show me and was so proud of himself. Of course, we made a big deal and were so excited.

- As long as your toddler is really ready, shows interest, and stays calm and happy when you try with him, it can be a good time to make the shift from diapers. When his diaper is dry for long periods of time during the day, catching him in time to go in the potty can be fun for him and for you. That's what we did. The main thing is not to stress. Get a good book about it, and don't worry.

When your child uses the bathroom, he will need help to wipe his bottom. He might miss and wet the toilet seat. When this happens, be encouraging: "That's good you were trying. You remembered to hold your shirt up." Over time, he will gain competence. The next time he tries, you can say, "That's great. You went in the toilet! You made good progress." Help your child to move confidently in small steps toward his goals—and celebrate his efforts. Importantly, when your child sees you responding with patient kindness and flexibility, he can relax and take pride in his progress.

Getting children to try new foods and eat balanced meals can be another parenting challenge. A mother with two children said, "Jack only has a few foods he really likes to eat. Most of them involve peanut butter. We eventually 'ran out' of peanut butter and cut back on in-between meal snacks. We began serving him just a bit of what we were having. Finally he really was hungry and began to add new foods to his diet."

> Stay with children when they need assistance. Talk through the process. Encourage and cheer small steps in the right direction.

The goal is to nurture a healthy relationship with food and the body, helping children to feed themselves with love and respect. Teach children to "eat what your tummy tells you," and to "listen to your tummy." Staying in tune with their body's needs is an important skill. Following are other tried-and-true approaches for resolving mealtime struggles:

- **Offer food at mealtimes.** Instead of handing over snacks when children are bored, offer a book, a game, or other activity.

- **Enjoy your own food.** If you want your children to eat something, enjoy it with them. Your modeling is the strongest indicator of what children will eat.

- **Offer just a bit on the child's plate.** It may be tempting to say, "Just try a little." But then you have a power struggle. Include a bit on the plate without comment.

- **Take small steps in the right direction.** If you have gotten in the habit of yogurt every day for breakfast and mac and cheese every night for dinner, gradually introduce new foods one at a time. For example, add cut-up apples instead of chips to your child's lunch.

- **Honor individual texture preferences.** Keep in mind that young children can be sensitive to texture. For example, some children like their broccoli crunchy; others like it soft. If children have trouble with a certain food, introduce it again in a week or so.

- **Offer a variety.** Children who are exposed to a wide variety of healthy foods develop a preference for these. With food allergies, many substitutions are available, such as replacing wheat noodles with gluten-free brown-rice pasta, quinoa, or soft-cooked potato cubes. Be sure to talk with your pediatrician about what is right for your child.

- **Ensure true hunger.** Children who are active with aerobic exercise—meaning they are running and playing—naturally self-regulate eating patterns. Be sure to provide plenty of fresh water between meals.

It is critical to refrain from power struggles over food. Saying, "Have a bit of this before you can have that . . ." is a way of controlling what a child eats. Instead, just say, "When you are hungry, you can eat." Be sure the food on the plate is what your pediatrician recommends for the age of your child.

Share your own love of cooking by letting your child watch and help you cook. Older children who participate in shopping and cooking learn to develop a life-long interest in healthy cooking and eating. Try putting your preschooler or school-aged child in charge of planning, shopping, and cooking with you one night a week. With your assistance, new skills and interests will develop.

Getting Support for Positive Behavior

We were putting Mei Ling to sleep each night at 8:00 p.m., walking her back and forth during her fussy time. Finally, we said, "Let's keep track of the real amount of time she fusses, because it seems like a lot." We realized she was fussy for exactly one hour. We backed up her bath time to 6:00 p.m. and put her to bed at 7:00 p.m. It was shocking to realize that she had been fussy because she was tired. Moving up her schedule by one hour made all the difference.

When you see your child struggling with a transition, having difficulty sleeping, or needing extra support, look for regular patterns to understand what might improve the situation. Observing carefully can help you become aware of what is happening. Perhaps you are missing a solution that a simple evaluation can reveal.

For a baby, a cold may be on its way or a tooth getting ready to erupt, so keep in close contact with your pediatrician. For an older child, look for signs of fatigue, and make changes in sleep, the bedtime routine, or nutrition. You may find that meltdowns only happen after your child has played with a specific friend. Or perhaps you have been inconsistent, allowing a behavior sometimes but not others. Once you know what is happening, you can make the changes needed or give extra support at the appropriate time.

> Look for patterns that give clues and reasons, so that you find the best strategies, approaches, or solutions. What part of the environment, schedule, or interactions can you adjust?

Keeping a record can let you know if the issue really is happening as much as you think. Perhaps you can shift timing, adjust something in the environment, or prepare a child in a different way. You may find that your preschooler handles the morning better if you introduce table games and read with him before he plays alone. You may find that your toddler takes a longer nap if you take him outside first for fresh-air play. Often small modifications can make a big difference.

Once you discover what works best, communicate your expectations to the other adults in your child's life. Ask others who care for your child for their support to make it easier for your child to experience consistent expectations and routines. Set aside time to connect. Set a positive atmosphere and then say, "I want to share some goals that we have." With a family member, you can say, "We appreciate your role in Liam's life. You are so important to him. We are learning effective strategies for behavior guidance that we would like all of us to use together. These are approaches that we would like everyone who spends time with Liam to use." Share in writing the needed schedule, things to do with your child, and a brief list of rules and behavior expectations.

If someone responds, "We didn't raise our children like that," or "We don't do it like that," simply say, "It is wonderful to have lots of options for children and to know that there are many ways to parent. However, these are the specific things that are important to us. We are going to do these things at home and would like for you to do them when Liam is with you." It may help to say, "Why don't you try these for a few days, and if you have questions, just let us know. We are happy to support you in any way we can, and we don't mind talking about this again in a few days to see how everything is going."

If your child is in center- or home-based care, be sure to find out what kind of discipline and teaching system they use, and ask questions when you have concerns. A good sign of a positive experience is your child's own happy demeanor and response to daily routines and activities. The hallmark of quality care is open communication, the active role of parents, and a play-based environment with lots of nurture and positive encouragement for hands-on learning.

When your child begins pre-K or kindergarten, be sure to visit the classroom and school often and take an active part in parent events. If you are part of a home-school group, maximize opportunities available in your community. The more you understand the social and learning expectations, the more you will be able to provide caring and positive support at home. A strong partnership yields many benefits for your child, both in the present and in the years to come.

If you do not feel comfortable with a child care situation, trust your instincts. You know what is best for your child and can depend on your perceptions and feelings. When you have concerns, don't wait to communicate. If a serious issue cannot be resolved, look for a caregiving experience that is a better match. Your child's well-being and best interest are your most important priority.

CHAPTER 8
BUILDING
CHARACTER

Instilling Positive Values

I want my children to have a strong identity, high self-esteem, and love. I want them to have integrity. But I worry about focusing so much on the daily things that I miss the chance to leave a lasting legacy in their lives.

What would you write to your children if you gave them a letter filled with your life wisdom? Perhaps you would write, "It's not about money, having the latest technology, or getting good grades. There are deeper qualities and core values that matter." All of us have beliefs that give our lives purpose and that reflect our identities. Like a family flag or crest, your children will become known for your unique family traits. This often happens without much thought, by passing down what was modeled to us. However, when you make passing the baton a priority, you can nurture these values more purposefully.

If you were asked to share the top three traits you want for your child, what would they be? If you are outgoing and have good people skills, you might say a good sense of humor, friendliness, and the ability to get along with others. If you enjoy adventure, you might say perseverance, the love of learning, and a willingness to take risks. Maybe you want your child to be creative and to use this gift to solve problems. Often the traits we value are like our own—or those wish we had. Most parents want their children to have empathy and integrity. They hope their children will have courage to speak up for the needs and rights of themselves and others and look for the good in and bring out the best in others. Parents want their children to have a deep sense of character that can guide their lives.

Educator Maria Montessori suggested that character comes from experience and not from explanation. Children absorb our values by watching the way we respond to daily life. When they see us help someone put groceries into the car, they understand that helping matters. When they see that we are gentle toward ourselves and respect our own needs, children learn that it is natural to nurture and respect themselves, too. What we live and bring them alongside to experience with us will be what they believe to be true.

Many of us rekindle a faith tradition when we become parents. Robert Coles, child psychiatrist and professor at Harvard University, is a Pulitzer Prize–winning writer and author of *The Spiritual Life of Children*. He suggests that children's spiritual curiosity and interest in faith are a part of natural development that provides wholeness and cohesion. He proposes that listening and being sensitive to children's questions and wonderings can teach us a great deal about their inner lives. By letting them lead the conversation, we can encourage the strength of their inner compass.

According to Claire Lerner and Lynette Ciervo, authors of "Parenting Young Children Today: What the Research Tells Us," two-thirds of parents surveyed say their faith or religious background has a major or moderate influence on their approach to child rearing. People feel strongly about building spiritual and moral understanding about responsibility toward others, instilling democratic ideals, and building character traits that can guide children's decisions in life. Those who value their own rich faith experiences often want their children to experience the same beliefs, songs, and traditions. Those without a faith practice often desire for their children to have a strong moral and cultural grounding, and may seek a faith experience for the first time as part of raising their child. Most parents want their children to internalize strong integrity and character and seek out others who can be role models for these qualities.

Consider the character qualities you most admire. Seek friends who exemplify these characteristics and who will encourage you to make personal growth a priority. Take the time to say, "I admire the way you live your life. How did you develop these traits in yourself and your children?" You can learn so much from the viewpoints and experiences of others. When you open yourself to the input of others who care about you, you will grow and deepen your perspective in powerful ways.

When children develop joy in giving to others, they want to experience this feeling again. They learn that their special gifts and talents matter. They look for ways to encourage others and are excited to put their interests into action. Their early experiences often become the root of wonderful passions that will last long into their adult lives.

Activating Empathy

My three children, all under age five, seem to have a sixth sense about my expectations and intentions. They can tell that I trust them and so are likely to do the right, kind, and gentle thing. They know what I think— whether it is in my voice or body language. So I keep my relationship with each child positive. Every time I notice their caring, I hug them and respond immediately. I may not see changes today, but they are making progress.

Empathy is the ability to feel with others and the desire to reach out and help. Empathy in action is compassion. It has boosting power to help children enjoy closer relationships with others and self-reinforces as it gives back deep feelings of satisfaction. A mom of three children said, "My boys get excited about a bowl of crackers. They run and sit on the porch to eat them and talk. When my four-year-old spilled his and there weren't any more, my three-year-old offered to share his bowl. I could see he already had a deep sense of empathy."

Children are naturally caring and express their feelings genuinely. When they see someone upset, they instinctively want to give comfort. Even babies in the hospital will cry when they hear other babies crying. An older baby will offer his pacifier to another who is crying. Empathy is an inborn trait, but putting it into action consistently requires support.

Expose your child to role models who are passionate about their work. Take piano lessons yourself and watch your child absorb your love for music. Eat well and exercise, and watch your child imitate your example. Don't just talk about a character quality. Live it.

By the age of four, children begin to understand that others have feelings that differ from their own. This involves the ability to reflect on one's own thoughts and feelings and the ability to tune in to the feelings of others. This doesn't always result in the ability to put the needs of others before one's own. But as they enter the grade-school years, children become more consistent in using empathy to guide their decisions.

All children struggle at times with frustration and may act impulsively by snatching things, teasing, or having difficulty sharing. It takes time and effort to help children identify their feelings and to react in ways that help themselves and others. They need ongoing adult support to gain consistency. The following strategies can boost empathy in young children:

> Teach children to look out for the feelings and needs of others. Talk frequently about the effects of words and actions, and consider the perspectives of others. Take children along with you to do caring deeds and random acts of kindness that help others.

- **Guard your words.** Demonstrating empathy toward yourself and others is one of the most powerful messages you can send. When things go wrong, you can say, "Oh, that is so sad, but I will know better how to do it next time." The message you give is, "I may feel frustrated now, but I am in control of myself and my attitudes." In contrast, if you complain or are self-critical, you teach your children that that you are the victim of your circumstances and your mistakes.

- **Model language about feelings.** Describing our own and others' emotions helps children recognize and interpret feelings. "I feel sad when Jordan is sick." "We feel excited when Grandma is coming." "Daddy is smiling. He is so happy when we help him carry his things." Noticing and understanding emotions is the first step in responding to them.

- **Validate rather than contradict feelings and perceptions.** When a child says, "It's hot in here," you may feel like responding, "No, it's not. You're just hot from running." Instead of denying the child's perception, teach her to trust her thoughts and perceptions. It is better to respond, "Yes. Your face is flushed—I can see you look hot. Do you want to put on a T-shirt?" Build acceptance and respect for what is true.

- **Encourage creative dramatic play.** Researchers Deborah Leong and Elena Bodrova, as well as Sue Waite and Sarah Rees, have found that dress-up and imaginative play increase empathy and sensitivity to others. Dramatic play lets children take on other roles and consider the perspectives of others. Providing simple costumes and props helps children act out stories and practice social skills.

- **Reduce children's stress.** Children experience positive stress from the excitement of being a goalie in a soccer game, taking a test, or hurrying to get somewhere on time. In these everyday events, they can recover quickly. To help your child handle stress positively, teach skills such as talking through the steps of preparation: "Before the game, I can stretch, focus on the play, and support my team." Children who can calm themselves can focus on the needs of others.

- **Model stress-reducing strategies.** Show your children how you negotiate your own stress: "I am going to take a few deep breaths to calm down." "Let me have a few minutes to think about what I want to do." When children see you thinking before you act, they learn that this strategy can make good things happen.

- **Make thinking visible.** Self-reflection by adults invites children to engage in more thoughtful ways of responding. "Even though I want to get my work done, I understand how much Mia needs my help right now." "Even though I was going to sort this pile, I can wait and finish this work later." Talk out loud about what you are thinking when you make good choices.

- **Draw attention to others' feelings.** Awareness is the first step in empathy. "Put yourself in his shoes. How do you think that made him feel?"

- **Model forward-thinking strategies.** Think aloud before you react. "I wonder what I could say to make this situation turn out well?" "What words could I choose that will make both of us happy?"

A child with a caring heart is able to give and receive empathy and love. When you make this trait a priority, amazing changes happen. Talk more often about what a difference one person can make in the world. Be empathetic toward your children, and they, in turn, will stay more connected to you.

Encouraging Kindness

When I want my children to be kind, I try to catch them being sweet to each other. "It's so kind to help your sister clean up. It's a two-person job. You can get it done faster when you work together." By talking about the reasoning behind it, the message makes more sense.

Kindness needs attention to grow. Children are generally truly caring and express their love for others genuinely. They want to do what they can to help. When children are young, nurture this desire to be kind to others by letting them know that what they do makes a difference. You can talk about what kindness means and why it matters. Here are some descriptions of kindness offered by five- to eight-year-old children:

- Letting our friend choose the music or game when we are playing

- Giving our friend the first choice of food, where to sit, or where to sleep when she comes over

- Helping someone when you don't feel like putting down your book to do it

- Setting the table to show your mom kindness when she has a lot to do

- If someone is being mean, saying something nice and taking a friend away to play

- If someone is crying, bringing a tissue and staying with them until they feel better

- Sharing your sandwich if someone forgets their lunch

As the authors related in our article "Is Tattling a Bad Word? How to Help Children Navigate the Playground," research suggests that adults often make excuses for unkindness by saying, "She didn't mean it," or "He must have been tired." However, writing off what happened teaches a strong lesson that sometimes it's okay to be rough or insensitive with our words or actions if we aren't feeling great at the moment. Take opportunities to make your children aware of ways to be kind. When you see television characters laughing at the expense of others, point it out: "I am surprised everyone laughed at the girl. How do you think she felt? How would you feel?" Talk about what that person could have done or said to be kind instead. Being kind when others are not takes determination.

Sometimes, families can get into the habit of making fun in ways that they feel are harmless. It is easy to say, "Did you see the funny shoes Aunt Millie wore?" without thinking about the pattern that sets. If you disagree with a politician or neighbor, say, "Sometimes, people have different ideas." You can share your point of view or defend your opinions without saying unkind things about the other person. But it is better to save the "hot topic" comments for adult conversations when children are not present.

> Let children overhear you speaking positively about them, pointing out their good qualities, efforts, and actions. Children will live up to your opinions.

Children notice the differences between themselves and others. They have a natural curiosity about their own and others' races, ethnicities, socioeconomic status, and other differences. Rather than wait until after you hear negative words or witness exclusion, actively talk about these topics with sensitivity and understanding.

When children are kind, describe what they did. Let others hear about the great things you observe. "You were quick to share with your brother." "Thanks for waiting to help your dad today." Your affirmations have the power to build up confidence.

Inspiring Courage

> *My son was with me at the deli counter and saw that the crawfish were on special. He said, "Dad, it's only $2.00 for a crawfish. Can I get one and eat it at home?" I thought, "This is a waste of time and money." But I wanted to encourage him to try new things and to think outside of the box. So we bought one and cooked it, and he ate it. My son still talks about it. He still likes to take positive risks to reach new goals. I think of this as the "crawfish decision." It was a great investment.*

To prepare children for the teen years ahead, instill habits that will keep them safe and help them make good decisions. You want them to try new things that are positive yet say no when offered a destructive choice. Often, this will require courage. Truthfully, it's a scary world. Children need to be allowed to take risks, and parents will eventually have to turn responsibility over to them—but fear can influence our thinking.

Rather than giving in to "snow plow" parenting—moving all of the obstacles out of the way—let your children try things out and learn from their mistakes. Life is full of challenges, and you want things to work out well. How do you decide what risks are needed? Here are some strategies to help you strengthen your children's confidence:

- **Set goals.** Encourage your children to try new things. At school, they can aim for more words correct on a spelling test, improvement on running in gym, or figuring out something new in math. No one is always good at doing new things right away. Children have to learn and get stronger in their skills as they practice.

- **Talk about courage.** You can't expect children to always succeed. Let them know it's okay to fail. Children need to be brave enough to tell the teacher something is wrong or ask for what they need. They have to be strong enough to tell a friend that she's making a wrong choice or to stick up for someone who needs support. There are times they need to stand up for what is right—even when others disagree. Some things may not turn out as you want, and you have to assure your child can she can come home and talk to you about what happened.

- **Troubleshoot ahead of time.** When your child is facing a new environment, talk about what she might face. For example, going to a new school can be scary. Talk with your child about her fears and what to expect: "You have to ride the bus. What do you think that will be like?" "Tell me how you are feeling about school? What else will be scary?" Your child may say, "I don't know where I am going. I don't know the people. I won't know the answers." Give reassurance. "The children you will meet are your future friends." "No one knows the answers before they go to school to learn." Talking ahead of time relieves anxiety.

- **Talk openly about children's fears.** Young children are often afraid to go to the doctor or worry about getting a shot. They may be afraid other children will make fun of them at school or at sports practice. A birthday party may make some children feel anxious. They may not want to play a new party game or may be nervous about finding their way in a strange house. They may be afraid of expectations in music, art, or gym. Talk about what to do when they face something new.

- **Problem solve.** Help your children think ahead about how they will handle challenges. Ask, "What would you do? What would be the right thing if your friends tell you to take a pack of gum?" Then practice answers: "No, we don't have money for that. We can't take that without paying." Practice helps children do the right thing, even when others pressure them and even when no one else is looking.

- **Expose your children to heroes**. Read stories about people or characters who have made positive choices and demonstrated courage. Invite people to dinner who work in helping fields, such as military service members, police, medical workers, or fire fighters. When guests are visiting, ask them to share how they need courage in their work or lives. Reading about heroes can accomplish the same goal.

Courage comes when you transfer responsibility to your children and help them practice. The time to start strengthening these skills is now. One day, your little one will be a teen. Help her learn and understand the rules and take ownership of them. Then, when a friend says, "Hurry up and run the light," your child will have the courage to say, "Sorry. I am stopping."

When you talk openly with your children during the first eight years of life, they begin to view the world as a place where they can make a difference. They can connect their actions to consequences. They grow courage muscles and gain confidence, excitement, and pride in doing the right thing.

> Tell a story about a situation a child may encounter. For example, "There is a boy who found a wallet with money in it. He really wants to keep it. Should he (a) take it home, (b) turn it in to the school office, or (c) ask his friend what to do. What should the boy do?

Waiting Patiently

The one thing I wish my children would do is know how to wait. My three-year-old just said angrily, "I want what I want when I want," when her brother took her book. Waiting is not a strong point at our house.

Children often need to wait. They wait when you tell them you are going somewhere. They wait for their meals. They wait for the cookies to cool. They wait while you finish your phone conversations and wait while you run errands. It takes patience to put toys away, clean up after yourself, or finish one task before starting another. If you put an iPad in a child's hands the minute he needs something to do, you take away the chance for him to figure out how to quietly occupy himself. If you swoop in at every turn with toys, games, and snacks, you reinforce the idea that waiting is terrible. Life is full of waiting, so help your children learn to be creative and self-entertaining.

Young children are still developing inhibitory control. As related in his book *The Marshmallow Test,* in the 1960s at Stanford University's Bing Nursery School, researcher Walter Mischel and his students asked four-year-olds to refrain from eating a marshmallow for two minutes with the promise of getting a second one if they waited. Children who could wait were found to have a host of life benefits, all linked to the skill of waiting! Their ability to delay gratification predicted greater achievement in school, higher IQ, more happiness in life, greater stability, and better behavior. Reinforcing patience is one of the greatest gifts we can give. Help children learn about the benefits of waiting:

- Demonstrate how you are saving money by not buying something, so that you can afford to go to the zoo next month.

- Show how you bake cookies and put them away to share with company when they visit tomorrow, rather than eating the cookies now.

- Talk about the fact that you wait until you and the children get home from the store to eat, rather than passing around food in the car.

- Discuss that the children wait for Mommy or Daddy to come home before they open a package that has arrived in the mail.

- Remind them that they wait to see what is inside a birthday present until after their brother has opened it.

- Talk about how your family waits to eat until everyone sits down at the table, and you stay until everyone is finished.

- Point out that you can make positive conversation when you are in line at the car wash or at the store.

Teach your children that they can't have everything they want, and they can't always have what they want when they want it. Over time, they will begin to see that delay is okay and that good things come to those who wait. Show them that they can use their waiting time to earn what they want: "I like that Lego set, too. I think that would be a good one for you. Why don't you help me in the yard each weekend, and we can put the money in a jar? When you have enough, you can buy the Lego set." Learning to wait and working toward a goal are important parts of growing up.

For young children, cues can help them remember to wait. Toddlers love to make a "patient hat" by pointing their fingers over their heads. Older children can learn finger exercises to entertain themselves or can read a hand cue from their parents to remind them of how many minutes they need to wait. This is a kind and respectful way of reminding them of the need to be patient.

As children learn that their needs will be met, they will be able to wait for longer periods of time. They will need to wait as teenagers—for a car, to earn the money to buy something, to have more autonomy. Having practice in waiting during early childhood gives them confidence that they are in control over the decisions they make.

> Give your children a cue to remind them—ahead of time—of the behavior you want them to exhibit. Let them know you appreciate their patience.

Ensuring Honesty

I tell my boys, "I can always count on you to tell the truth." When they are together in the yard and their friends are talking all at once about a problem, I say, "I am so glad you will tell me what happened." And they do.

Integrity means acting with honesty and keeping your word, whether you are alone or in the company of others. It means being authentic in your dealings and living by the Golden Rule—treating others as you want to be treated. Help children be honest by thanking them when they tell the truth. Even if they need to clean up a mess or pay back the cost of a broken item, they can be sure that you will be kind and respectful when they are honest.

It can be reassuring to know that higher intelligence is related to children's ability to manufacture creative stories, as Stephanie Lu points out in her article "From Lying Children to Successful Adults." When children are young, they may simply have vivid imaginations and tell you fantastic tales about the elves that came at Christmas or the magic fairy that lives in the back yard. This isn't lying; it is part of normal imaginative play. A great response is, "Oh, I love your imagination! I am happy you are thinking of beautiful elves. Thank you for telling me." It is best to accept their understanding and sense of fun.

If your child is not truthful, however, what researchers have learned about lying can help you be thoughtful in the way you respond. According to researchers Victoria Talwar, Cindy Arruda, and Sarah Yachison, the most common reason children lie is to avoid punishment, so use these situations to teach rather than punish. By the time children are three or four, they want to protect themselves from getting punished. Even when a parent has seen a behavior, a child may be afraid and say, "I didn't take it," or "I didn't hit her." Research by Victoria Talwar and Kang Lee shows that children can understand the difference between truth and lying around the age of three, and so it is important to talk about how good it feels to tell the truth and how you value and respect telling the truth. Show your understanding: "I know it is hard to admit when you did something wrong." And children don't grow out of lying, so take every opportunity to reinforce and thank your children for telling the truth.

Often children will make up explanations for something that happened out of fear of the consequences. One mom said, "My seven-year-old daughter needed stitches after she bashed into the side of the swimming pool with her chin. She was afraid she had done something wrong and told the doctor she had been pushed. She said she was afraid the doctor would be mad at her." Reassure your children that accidents happen and that it is okay to tell what really happened.

In a research study by Angela Evans and Kang Lee, children were asked not to peek into a box. Many later told a lie if they had been unable to keep themselves from peeking. They didn't want the researchers to know they did not obey the request. Children may not have the self-control to refrain from doing something they are asked not to do. They may feel bad about it and fear a parent's anger or an adult's disappointment.

To encourage honesty, ask questions that invite cooperation: "How did this happen? Can we clean this up together?" Instead of asking, "Did you do this?" simply say, "I am sorry that this happened. I am sure you feel terrible. Can you hold the bag for me while we clean it up?" Bringing your child alongside you to help invites her to tell you what really happened.

Rather than accusing, simply describe what you see:

- "The playdough is all over the floor. Here is the whisk broom and dust pan."

- "I see scribbles on the wall. Please color on paper. Let's clean up the wall. Here is a sponge for you to use, and I can use this one."

- "I can see that both you and your sister are upset. What can you do to fix this so that you are not frustrated?"

Blaming invites defensiveness and arguing; whereas, asking for a solution invites problem solving and instills personal responsibility. When you suspect a child did not comply with a request or you actually see her doing something that is off limits, don't ask a question about which you already know the answer. It is better not to set her up to lie. Instead of asking, "Did you take a cookie?" you can ask, "Did you have difficulty doing what Daddy asked? Next time, we will put the cookies up high until after dinner." Creating teaching moments instead of making accusations makes a lasting impression.

Remember that shame keeps a child from focusing on the lesson and shifts her body and mind to awareness of embarrassment. Instead, talk about the difference between right and wrong, and help her respect others' boundaries and belongings. The teaching moment will transfer responsibility and create greater success in the future, because it helps the child focus on the lesson at hand.

Ensuring a nonpunitive response when a child tells the truth reinforces honesty. If a child says, "I broke the vase," and then gets punished, of course she is more likely to lie the next time she breaks something. Instead, talk with her about what to do when she breaks something. "It feels terrible when we break something that belongs to someone else. Let's be extra careful not to touch." As children get older, they can make age-appropriate amends. For example, a child can do extra chores to earn money to replace her sister's broken toy. Restitution should be made as a matter of responsibility, not as a matter of punishment.

> Support your partner's decisions. It helps to check with each other before you talk to a child about a specific incident, so that you won't be giving different messages.

To encourage honesty, set the example. Think about what your child sees. If, for example, you eat food in the grocery store before it is paid for or forget to ask before you borrow something that belongs to your child or spouse, you are setting an example that you wouldn't want your child to follow. Be careful to behave in ways that show respect for others and honesty. Here are some other important ways to reinforce honesty:

- **Give honest complements.** Teach your child to say something true about a gift received, such as, "It was so thoughtful of you to bring me a present," rather than, "I love the shirt," when you really don't love it. When your child hears you make a negative comment about the shirt later, she will know you weren't telling the truth.

- **Honor real feelings.** To a toddler who has just smacked grandma on the arm when she tries to take away a toy, refrain from saying, "Tell Grandma you love her." Instead say, "It's okay to tell Grandma you want to keep the toy, but it's not okay to hit." To Grandma, say, "I am sorry Tommy got frustrated and hit. He is working on using his words." Remember that the child may not understand why he needs to relinquish the toy. Say, "We need to come to dinner. Shall we put the toy on the shelf or in the box?"

- **Model the truth.** Instead of saying someone is not home when the phone rings, simply say, "I am sorry, John can't come to the phone right now," or "John is home but will be returning his calls in about an hour. May he call you then?"

- **Give honest reasons**. If you haven't completed a task on time, rather than saying, "I already did it," and scrambling to get it done, or saying, "I was late because of traffic," tell the truth. People appreciate honesty: "I am behind on that project. I'm working to complete it today," or "I just couldn't get organized. I'm sorry I'm late."

- **Model taking responsibility.** Rather than blaming someone or something else, own up to your part. For example, say, "I am really sorry. I broke the knob on the toaster when I twisted it too hard. Can it be glued back on?" instead of saying, "That cheap toaster broke."

- **Teach responsibility for oneself.** Let your children decide whether they are hungry enough to eat more or comfortable enough to give someone a hug. Rather than saying, "Give Aunt Mildred a hug goodbye," simply say, "Let's wave goodbye!" Offering hugs or words of love and deciding amounts of food to eat—these boundaries belong to children. Teach children that it is their job to listen to their bodies and make good decisions for themselves. This honest connection to self and trust of one's own feelings keeps sensitivity strong.

It takes practice to be an honest person. Honesty grows like a seed, with nurturing, sunlight, weeding, and staking when support is needed. It grows in the small places first and sets down deep roots that will hold when challenges come. It takes determination to show children that it is okay to not be perfect and that everyone makes mistakes. Even more, children need to hear you owning up to the truth. They then learn there is no shame in telling the truth, even when it reveals weakness. Teach your children that you love them unconditionally and that it is okay to fail or make mistakes. They can ask for help rather than continue to feel trapped in trying to live up to expectations.

Practicing Gratitude

I was constantly correcting my children: "How can you say that nicely? Ask in a polite tone of voice." I was grouchy, and they were grouchy. I knew we needed a happiness shift to turn around our mood. So, I listed everything I could think of that I felt thankful for: my husband's blue eyes, my daughter's curly hair, my son's silly laugh, the yummy sandwich we were eating. And then I asked them what they were thankful for. They said they were thankful for me. The conversation only lasted a minute, but it changed everything.

Life contains plenty of opportunity to feel disappointment and frustration. It is not likely that every day will be filled with pure contentment and satisfaction. But your words can play an active role in shaping the direction of your feelings. Finding ways to speak positively can plant the seeds of gratitude, encourage others, and boost the power of positivity in your life.

Do you sound contented with what you have? Do you sound grateful for even the little things? Let your children hear you speaking words of gratitude. An attitude of gratitude will spread a blanket of reassurance to those around you and set a positive tone for your children. You may have heard that today's children feel entitled to have things come easily to them. The remedy for entitlement is to experience a deep sense of gratitude for what you have. Gratitude is a habit that you can actively cultivate with your children.

When grumbling thoughts or negative self-indulgence threaten to set in, replace those patterns with joyful gratitude. Here are some ways to do this together:

- **Give thanks.** Whatever your faith background, offer a prayer or statement of gratitude at meals. This shared tradition will take your thoughts from the busy pressures of the day and help you focus on family time and thankfulness for the food and comforts you have.

- **Make a thankfulness chain.** Each time someone in the family is loving or kind or says something special about someone else, add a link to a paper chain. When the chain reaches across the room, celebrate with a picnic in the park or an afternoon at the library.

- **Plan thankfulness shares.** Let your children sort through their toys as they grow up or move on from certain dolls, building sets, or books. Make a giveaway basket for a younger sibling, for a family in need, or to offer as a donation to a children's organization. Nothing fills the heart with thankfulness more sweetly than joy that is shared.

- **Describe what thankfulness looks like.** Children are often given general requests such as, "Be nice to your friends," "Use nice words," and "Be thankful." Children may have no real idea of what is expected. Talk about what it means to be truly thankful.

- **Write thank-you notes.** Don't wait to receive a gift. Help your child write a note to his teacher or to someone for whom he is thankful. Toddlers and preschoolers can draw pictures and will love helping you fold and tuck their gift into an envelope before you address it to the person.

- **Keep a family thankfulness journal.** At dinner, ask each person to tell something they are grateful for or the best thing that happened to them that day, and record these thoughts. As children learn to write, they will enjoy being the thankfulness writer.

- **Give compliments.** When siblings struggle, have each one say two kind things about the other for which they are thankful. Everyone at the dinner table can say a compliment about the person next to them.

- **Keep a thankfulness jar.** Tuck in notes when special things happen. Children will love to put notes in, too. Read the notes together at the end of a week. Some families do this each day in November and read the notes at Thanksgiving. You will find that you really are counting your blessings.

- **Share sweet dream wishes.** At the end of each day, whisper what you are thankful for. This can be a prayer or a simple conversation. "Doesn't this warm, cozy bed feel perfect?" "I am so grateful for the fun we had at the store together." "It was great making dinner for Grandpa." "Falling asleep to the beautiful lullaby music will bring sweet and happy dreams to your heart." Whispered words of thanks are magic to the ears.

Thankfulness is a lens through which you can view every situation. "I guess we are stuck in traffic. That gives us time to plan our weekend. Do you want to go to the slide park or the climbing park?" Rather than frustration, your child will remember your sweet time together.

> Explain what is needed in a positive way, and give children opportunities to succeed. Be sure you tell the child right away how much you value and appreciate what she has done.

Helping Others

From the time they were in preschool, we took our three children to sing at their grandmother's retirement home. The first year, they were scared and didn't want to go. But when all of the people clapped and shook their hands and thanked them, a tradition was born. They still talk about the first time they went and how proud they are to go.

When you include your children in giving to others—baking and sharing cookies with a neighbor, getting the mail for someone who is sick, making a meal for a family in need—they learn the habit of giving. Children who give appreciate and value what they have. They see that others need help and learn that giving can be a way of life.

Generous people feel joy in making the day go better for others, smiling at the person who helps them at the store or assisting someone in the parking lot. Habits of giving need practice to make them grow. Children don't always understand the time, effort, and skill others have given to help them. They don't see the planning and energy that goes into a task. When they participate in the steps of giving, they gain perspective. Putting aside time to participate with parents in community service can have a lifelong impact. Here are some ways to help your child start helping others:

- Surprise a parent, sibling, or relative with a random act of kindness. You and your child could fold their clothes, make their bed, do their chore, or bring a book from the library they would love.

- Buy a food item to place in the food-pantry box at the grocery store, church, or charity organization.

- Help your child choose a toy or clothing to give away.

- Include your children when you serve a meal, donate used clothing, or pick up litter in the community.

- Make cards or collect stuffed animals for children at a hospital or hospice.

- Fill holiday care boxes for children, including new toothbrushes, personal items, and small toys, for a charity organization or local food pantry.

- Help neighbors by bringing in their mail or feeding the cat when they are away.

- Run an errand for someone in need.

- Deliver food or needed items to a neighbor.

- Participate in a walk-a-thon or other charity event. Even a young child can participate in a stroller.

- Draw a get-well picture or write a letter to mail to a sick friend.

Children are natural helpers. Elicit the child's support by asking her to help you out. Helping others releases joy and increases the bonds of connection.

Children may not feel like giving at first, but encouraging them to do the unexpected can be fun. At home, an older sibling can surprise a younger one by helping clean her room or assisting her with homework. Children can be generous when a sibling or parent is sick and can take care of the dog or do another chore. Making breakfast in bed for a parent and leaving special notes can be a tradition that encourages family fun and bonding—while teaching the joy of helping others.

Catching on to Cooperation

I have learned to be very careful about the things that I say will or will not happen, because it is easy to lose track of what I have promised. The most important lesson I have learned is to keep my promises. My children know they can rely on me, so I only make commitments that I can keep. I have to think first before I say something and know whether I can actually do it.

You cannot choose what your children will be or what they will love to do. But when you are passionate about your own life and invest enthusiastically in activities you care about, your children will see and understand the deeper meaning in your actions. There are specific ways you can influence your children's outlook:

- **Replace negative thoughts with positive truths to boost confidence.** Instead of saying, "I can't do this!" try, "I might not know how to do this now, but I will get help and figure it out!"

- **Anticipate resistance to change.** Have fun and be intentional. Listen carefully to the words that you say! If you catch yourself focusing on the negative, quickly reframe your words to the positive goals you want to live. It takes time to build new habits.

- **Recognize that children watch and listen.** Your children take their cues about how to treat themselves and others by the way you treat and talk to them. Be purposefully patient.

- **Be an encourager.** Make interesting conversation and laughter in normal, everyday situations. Show contentment rather than acting entitled. Teach that it's okay to be sad but not to have self-pity. Step away from comments that make you a victim, and focus on making good things happen.

- **Plan what to do when things don't go well.** Remember what is important. Don't make decisions when you are tired; wait until morning when you can think clearly. Perspective is everything.

> Remember that everyone needs to feel that she belongs and is significant. Help each child feel important by giving her important jobs to do and reminding her that if she doesn't do them, they don't get done! Help her feel important by being responsible.

- **Encourage pitching in.** Beware of becoming a "do for" parent, and keep encouraging your children to do for themselves and others by using their abilities to contribute. Helping others instills a lasting sense of significance.

When you invite your children to contribute in ways that matter, they begin to see themselves as important to the lives of those around them. They develop pride in the teamwork they feel and experience the joy of cooperating with others they love. Children love helping with plans, organizing activities, making decisions, and taking part in events. Over time and with your support, they will gain positive habits and leadership that become part of their thinking and lives.

In the everyday moments, you have opportunities to instill positive character traits and to help children become cooperative, compassionate, generous, creative, and caring. Your investment will help your children internalize respect for themselves and others. You can inspire courage and leave a lasting legacy of integrity in your children's lives.

CHAPTER 9
BEING YOUR BEST SELF

Creating a Family Identity

Both of us work from home and have a high amount of accountability for our jobs. We both travel several days a month, as well. No matter what, we always sit down for dinner together on Thursday evenings. We plan our food, the shopping, and what we will do with the children on the upcoming weekend. We never skip it. Because of this, we have really begun to incorporate fun day trips and activities. We can see a difference in our children's behavior during the week, because they are looking forward to our time together. We keep a strict bedtime schedule with bath, reading, and bed. We have to sleep to handle work—so we are all in bed by 8:00!

From the time babies are born, most families try to fill their children's lives with the nurturing and love they need. Parents teach, train, explain, and begin the process of transferring responsibility for their children's lives to their children. Families lay the foundation for the decisions and challenges children will face in the years ahead. As a parent, you can feel confident when you know that you are focusing on your children's most important need—building a strong and healthy connection with you.

Work to create a unique identity for your family in which you really enjoy each other. One mom said, "We want all of our children to appreciate music, whether they play an instrument or not. We play music and dance together at every birthday party." Creating traditions unique to your family can create special memories of fun. Your distinctive personalities and interests will influence your style. Here are some ideas to get started:

- **Make a family symbol for your "team."** Create T-shirts with a unique image for each family member. Make up your own logo or family crest. These can be made with paints, markers, or handprints. This sense of identity says, "We are Team (your last name)."

- **Have fun with creative ideas for birthdays and holidays.** One family shared, "We make ornaments for the grandparents with the children's pictures. The children make their own cards. It doesn't cost much, and we do this each year to begin the holiday season."

- **Enjoy a special family meal each week.** Try spaghetti night with Italian music on Saturdays, with an open invitation to family members. Whether it's pizza on Friday or a grilled cheese and tomato soup on Wednesday, it is the predictability that matters.

- **Institute Saturday- or Sunday-morning brunches**. Pancakes, waffles, omelets, or any other breakfast foods you like and a nicely set table can make a regular weekend morning into a special treat.

- **Hold an annual fall block party.** A fall event on your street or at the park with the neighbors can become an established ritual for the changing season, with potluck or grilling. Even very young children will sense the excitement.

- **Celebrate your heritage.** Tell stories about relatives' unique experiences, read books about children who share your roots, try recipes that pass on family traditions, and learn about musical styles that reflect your background.

- **Attend a church, synagogue or worship center, and make the drive or walk fun.** Several families shared, "We stop at my parents' every Sunday night and love hanging out with the cousins." "We get together with another family from our congregation at least once a month." "We meet other families for lunch or at the park after the service." Faith traditions can provide continuity and security. The extended community offers ongoing strength and support to growing families.

Wherever you live, you can maximize the fun. The park, zoo, community center, aquarium, local sledding hill, and your own back yard can bring magical experiences to your children. Spend an hour under a blanket on a hammock telling stories. Shovel snow and make a mini-sled run. Pack a picnic basket. Make a fort on the porch with sheets laid over a table. These experiences give siblings and friends lots of reasons to talk and laugh together.

Childhood adventures don't need to cost money. Camping out won't require fancy equipment. Roast marshmallows outside, and then have a slumber party in the living room. Take imaginary trips by reading stories about places around the world and deciding how you will travel there. If it is rainy, put on boots and turn the day into sunshine by taking a walk under an umbrella. Simple fun can form memories that your children will never forget.

If you work and your children are in the care of others, you can set aside time on the weekends to share a special activity together. Plan ahead for it or the day will slip by. Write invitations on cards for preschool or school-age children, and leave them on their pillows. Have a simple baking party to make muffins for breakfast. Help the children create seasonal place cards for a meal. It is the time you set aside to be together that matters.

A busy mom said, "My friend told me, 'Yeah, just take your child along with you, and not much will change after you become a parent.' I always wonder how she does that, when I am struggling just to get the routines together. I realize the trick is to enjoy activities myself and then share them with my child." Don't sit by and watch children have fun. Join in the play. If you love building, then enjoying blocks with your toddler makes sense. Erecting forts or constructing a back-yard cabin for pirate play gets school-aged children involved in planning and organization. If you are a fix-it kind of person, involve your preschooler in each step of household repairs. Write a list of materials needed, and take your child along to the hardware store. The process of sharing the task with children is the key.

> Family meetings give children an opportunity to plan, reflect, empathize, and problem-solve. Focus on two-way communication. Listen more than you talk. You will learn as much from your children as they do from you.

Plan a time each week to connect and talk together. When you gather around the table or cuddle on the couch, you can talk about what you have done and experienced and can share new ideas. Children can plan activities together for the weekend ahead. Setting aside family time helps children develop lasting pride in your family identity.

Keeping Your Goals in Mind

I often hear parents say, "I have a strong-willed child," like it is chicken pox or something else they wish their child didn't have. I have a strong-willed four-year-old. I want him to stand up and make a difference in the world. I want him to have the ability to say yes when something is good and no when it is harmful. My job is to teach him wisdom, so he can know the difference and put his energy to good use.

When things get crazy, children can get cranky. At those times, keep things simple. You can be purposeful and effective in turning things around. Here are tips to make those times easier for everyone.

- **Keep perspective.** Take a tip from the Disney song, and "Let It Go!"

- **Make chores fun.** When laundry in your child's room looks like an avalanche has hit, grab a large pail, basket, or container. Count items as you toss them in together. The message you will send is "Taking care of ourselves can be fun!"

- **Keep activity bags ready to go.** Fill a small sack with books, puzzles, drawing materials, chalk, pipe cleaners, a peg board and rubber bands, tiny cars, or little stuffed animals. Before a meltdown occurs, pass out a new activity. Children will learn to reach for it independently when they need something to do.

- **Let your child teach you.** Ask your child to show you how to set the table, fold a towel, build a tower, do a cartwheel, or sing a song. Taking the lead to teach a skill builds his knowledge and confidence.

- **Be patient.** Being part of a family can bring great joy. Laugh and enjoy each other. Kindness and patience set children up for success. Look carefully at your child's face before you speak, and see the need that is present. If you see a need for love, give a hug. If you see anxiety, reassure. If you see boredom, help engage him in something meaningful. If you see the need to connect, give your time. Every day, your child is doing his best and needs guidance and care.

Parents often teach children that, if they just do the right thing, good things will happen to them. But the truth is that life is hard. Prepare your children to handle the challenges and disappointments that they will face. Finding grace and joy in everyday experiences shows children how to find and create satisfaction. Your consistency and love can sustain them through remarkable and trying circumstances.

Positive relationships add layers of psychological strength. Grandparents, aunts and uncles, siblings, caregivers, teachers, and friends weave a lasting fabric of elasticity, encouraging children to stretch and to rebound from setbacks. Significant others instill trust and show children that their needs can be met in healthy ways. In spite of occasional bumps in the road, relationships can make the journey happy and satisfying.

The great thing about parenting is that parents are always learning, too. Children reflect their parents' guidance, so if you see an unwanted trait or habit in your child, consider that you may be the model for it. Think about your own actions, words, or attitudes, and try to model what you want your child to emulate. Our words have the power to influence children's responses. Make a mental note, determine to have a sense of humor, and keep growing.

At the heart of positive parenting is the honor you give to your children's spirits. At the same time, you guide them through new experiences and teach them the skills they need. Children who experience this kind of responsive parenting, in which authentic warmth and caring are present, feel respected and return that respect to others.

Navigating Adult Conflict

My husband often says to the kids, "We can't do it because we can't afford it." I tell him that I would rather he just say, "Let's go to the park (or something else) instead." I don't want them to worry all the time about money. We have learned we need to talk about what we want from each other.

Controlling your emotions is well worth the effort. Setting ground rules for handling differences and disagreements between adults can teach children needed lessons about conflict resolution. If you and your partner were raised in the same town and grew up together, conflicts may be fewer because you share a common upbringing and way of living. But if you are from separate geographical or ideological backgrounds, there may be greater differences. What do you believe about childrearing? How do you celebrate holidays? What are your feelings about money, spending, and saving? How do you divide the chores? How do you handle illness? You may think you are immune to conflict until your significant other does something that you find upsetting. Here are some tips to help:

- **Laugh together.** You are not the only ones to face challenges, and humor defuses a lot of frustration.

- **Retain some personal space.** Keep separate work spaces that you can manage in the ways that work best for you, even if it is simply a desk area.

- **Compromise.** Look for a common goal that you both can agree on. "I would prefer it to be neater, but I am okay with the mess if you straighten it up by Saturday." You are on the same team.

- **Beware of stockpiled frustration.** Even if something has been going on for a while, wait until you see it in the present before you bring it up: "I see the garage is left open when you drive the car in. It gets super cold in here. It will help so much for you to close the garage door each time."

- **Beware of assumptions.** Don't assume the other person knows what you want. You may secretly want your partner to do something without being asked. Asking directly gives a benefit to all. "I need help taking down the boxes. Would you be able to do it this afternoon or Saturday?" Positive choices work well in adult relationships, as well as in relationships with children.

- **Protect "me and you" time.** Try to set and keep a date once a week. You can stay at home or go out—but be sure you protect private connection time. This will give you opportunities to enjoy each other's company as well as to talk about significant issues.

- **Have discussions when you are rested.** Most discussions at night are less than productive because fatigue is a factor. Save needed planning and concerns for the bright morning sunlight over a cup of coffee and nice breakfast together.

- **Treat your family like company.** Keep an imaginary video camera running, so that you think before you speak. Remember how quickly positive words can turn feelings around.

- **Take needed space.** With minor disagreements, if you can make a quick decision, do so in front of the children. If you feel you need to revisit the issue, say, "Let's talk about this after we have had some time to think about it." This is a terrific way to model maturity to children.

- **Use "I" messages with your partner.** When you have a conflict, state the issue first, describe your feelings, and then give a positive and constructive suggestion for change. "When you leave the socks on the floor, I feel out of control, like I can't seem to stay on top of cleaning. I would like for you to pick them up and drop them in the bin. Would it help to put a basket by the bed?" Be patient and wait for a response. The answer is likely to be, "Okay. I can do that," or "Thanks for telling me."

With children, you can use this approach in a helpful way. "I notice you can't find what you need. Can we work together to get your papers organized or do you want to work on it alone?" Stick to the present. Keep it simple. Don't bring up past issues, and focus on a solution to the current situation.

> Own your feelings. Offer a positive suggestion for change. Stick to the present situation, and keep a caring connection open.

You don't want to tell a child that she has hurt your feelings when something doesn't happen the way you would like. Making a child feel guilty by leveraging your emotions removes boundaries, mucks up the picture about what is needed, and is manipulative. You don't want the child to change behavior because he feels coerced by your feelings or feels that changing his behavior will fix your feelings.

Help your children to think about the best ways to make life happen well. Frustrations give the opportunity to problem-solve and to take responsibility to make things better. Open communication is a healthy way to develop caring and sensitivity. It allows children to stay vulnerable and open to you and boosts both willingness and understanding.

Giving Encouragement

"What is wrong with you?" I muttered to myself when I knocked the toothbrush holder onto the floor. Then my two-year-old ran his truck into a bench. As he knocked over magazines, I said the same thing to him: "What is wrong with you, Michael? Watch where you're going!" The word wrong came out like an elongated, dramatic groan. At that moment, I had an incredible burst of insight. I realized that I was paying forward to him a dreadful message that I didn't want him to believe. I was determined to change it. Next time Michael made a mess, I asked, "Are you okay? Can I help you?" I knew I had to be the one to change.

Sometimes you may not be aware of how you sound. You may make a negative comment about something you did and not even pay attention to it: "Oh, I am always losing things. Where did I put that book?" That kind of statement communicates, "I am not very good at this." Reframe your words into productive statements. Instead of berating yourself, say, "I'll be careful when I find my book and put it on the table so that I can find it next time." Showing that you respect your own worth in spite of mistakes gives a strong message that children internalize.

For young children who are just gaining confidence in trying new things, having someone tell them they are capable—and then giving them opportunities to show it—can be life changing. Children need to hear, "You can do it." "It's going to be okay." "You can figure it out." If you say positive, encouraging words to them as they are developing new skills, they will soon repeat these affirmations to themselves.

> Give encouragement as often as possible. Positive words help children see how much they are growing and accomplishing.

It takes practice to get into the habit of giving positive feedback: "I like the way you arranged your blocks so carefully." "I appreciate how much time you spent drawing that picture." "Thanks so much for helping me pick up the trash. You are a great helper." "Can you help me with the glue? You are so good at fixing things." Not only do these messages make an indelible impression, but they reorient past negative messages.

Children love to see you come into the room when they know you are going to have fun, listen, and enjoy them rather than poking at something that is wrong. Your practice of affirmation sets the pace for your children as they talk to each other, as well. This approach creates a positive climate for your home. You can celebrate initiative, even when the results are still "in progress." You can be quick to say, "Doesn't it feel good to do that by yourself? You are getting better at this every day." How you encourage your child has a lasting impact.

Don't be surprised when things go wrong. After a night of little sleep, when your toddler makes a mess, the dog chews a favorite toy, and the baby is crying, leave everything—except for soothing the children and yourself. Later, you can come back and clean up the mess. It will still be there, waiting. The most important thing is how you make your children feel. In spite of minor disasters, look for the fun and funny things. Give lots of hugs, and let everything else go. These are the times that your children learn so much from you about how to live.

Enjoying Family Fun

What I wrote in my journal today: So long, toddler bed. Santa brought bunk beds! Our four-year-old is freaking out. As he runs down the hall and hurls himself on the mattress in a fit of excitement, I think, "Where did this time go?" Childhood is flying by.

Nurture your relationship with your child by building positive memories each day and fastening them together with strong cords of love and trust. Jump-start your success by writing out a list of fun activities that you want to do together with your child. Decide on a few places or events, and do some research on each one. Talk with your child about which one he is interested in doing. Plan ahead what to take with you, and read books about what you can learn while you're there.

Move beyond saying, "Go find something else to do." Make plans for constructive and interesting activities that are meaningful to you and your child. Start with a suggested activity and follow up with ideas of your own:

- **Cook dinner together.** Plan your own food-competition show, and plate the food beautifully. Children will love to place the layers of noodles for a lasagna and ladle in the sauce. Try a spiral vegetable peeler, and decorate your plates with healthy fruits and vegetables in the shapes of a scene or animal. There are many great cookbooks for kids that are simple and fun to use.

- **Have a kid-in-charge day.** The kid in charge can decide on meals, plan the grocery list, decide on chores, learn a new skill, or pick the movie-night movie. He can choose a special activity that the family can do together, decide who sits where at dinner, and enact any other fun ideas he can think of to make the day special.

- **Take up baking.** Make interesting family recipes together. The reading, measuring, and following directions provide a terrific learning opportunity with delicious rewards.

- **Hold a game night.** Make pizza, and let your children choose activities. Play board games, charades, word games, card games, or puzzles.

- **Make a memory book.** Take photos of your children doing activities they enjoy. Many online companies will print photo books for a minimal cost. Looking through your photo collections together is not only fun but will keep the memories fresh. Scrapbooking is another fun way to keep memories.

- **Take a family walk.** An after-dinner walk can become a treasured family tradition. The children can ride a bike, be pushed in a stroller, or pulled in a wagon. When your feet are moving, conversation is at its best.

- **Enjoy the outdoors.** Gather leaves, clip flowers, gather pinecone collections, plant an herb planter, or grow a salad garden. Start a minicompost pot and recycling center. Help your children see and experience nature as a place for active living.

- **Aim local.** Attend free open-air band concerts, craft events, or street fairs.

- **Get active.** With younger children, join a parent-child group for walking, dancing, or singing. Meet up with other parents once a week for a buggy brigade or dog walk. With older children, go roller skating, ice skating, sledding, bowling, or minigolfing.

- **Reach out.** Invite another family to come with you for a simple walk, bike ride, or trip to the park. A simple potluck meal shared together can jump start an ongoing tradition.

Set aside time to be together and share the fun. Make regular days into special days. When you are together in the kitchen grating and stirring, talking will come easily. Whether you bake, discover a recipe, prepare the ingredients, or simply share a special meal, when your hands are busy, your hearts will open up. Make a party out of an ordinary day and find ways to show how much you truly are thankful for your children, family, and friends.

> Celebrate the joy of family. Preparing food and cooking together provide wonderful ways to stay connected and build happy memories.

Understanding Your Children

Make sure you keep friends and others around who inspire you. Ignore the seemingly perfect lives posted on social media. Be with people who love to laugh and enjoy the day and who love you as you are.

Many people enjoy analyzing themselves. It can help to understand what makes you tick and can give better insight into your relationships. Do you like to take charge or step back and let someone else take the lead? Are you more open-ended and prefer to go with the flow, or are you happier when you plan things out in advance? Do you like to figure out what others need using intuition, or do you ask them directly about what they want?

> Leave "I love you" notes in surprising places. Tuck them in a shoe, next to the cereal bowl, or in a lunch. Tell children what you love about them.

Take a good look at your children, too. Your daughter may be outgoing and quick to try new things, or she may be analytical and prefer to wait to see what will happen before she steps in. Be a keen observer, and notice patterns of strength; it can help you become more effective in parenting your children. The key to nurturing a thriving child is to view both your own and your children's temperaments with respect and sensitivity. By responding gently to their needs as well as honoring your own, you can find a pattern and approach that works best for your family. Staying tuned in to your child and to yourself can help you understand the dynamics that are present.

You may want your child to be kind, caring, and have a sense of humor. You may hope he will be patient, sure of himself, and willing to take risks. You may want him to exhibit the best of your traits but maybe not the worst. Remind yourself that your children love unconditionally. They honestly love you as you are and look for that love in return.

Take time to tell your child what is special about him: a sense of humor, a sweet way of noticing what others need, or a knack for describing details in a beautiful way. Perhaps he can whistle and hum at the same time or turn fancy cartwheels and do made-up dances. Perhaps he is good at defending a point, is the first to notice when something is wrong, or is great at finding things. These are the qualities that may someday be assets for your children in their lives or careers. These are also the special reasons they are so dear to you.

Often, parents struggle the most with the child who is most like them. Or sometimes it is the child who is least like you who pushes your buttons. Recognizing similarities and differences can help you be more thoughtful in valuing your children and their unique traits.

Keeping Connections Strong

We don't talk down to the girls, and because of that they are respectful toward us and others. As long as we have respect for them, they feel it. They know that we care about their words and feelings. That will go just about as far as love will.

Whether you are home full time, working, or balancing multiple jobs, there are wonderful ways to stay connected to your child throughout the day. When you are together, you can give a hug or a quick back rub and spend time together. And there are many ways to remind your children that you are thinking of them when you are apart.

A working mom said, "I pick the children up at 5:00 p.m. at their grandmother's house on my way home. I always call them at 3:30. Hearing my voice and knowing I am coming soon makes the time hurry by. I set a certain time to talk to them even when I am out of town, and I never miss it. We use Internet video and talk about our day. The habit of connecting and the certainty that I am going to call them means a lot to me and to them. When I say goodbye in the morning, I always say, 'Talk to you at 3:30!' This is so reassuring to them."

Following are additional strategies that can help keep you connected:

- **Use reconnection time well.** Children are like puppies and want attention immediately—the minute you come home. By the time you have changed clothes and answered an e-mail, the prime time for young children will have passed. They need eye contact and focus the instant you walk in. If you have to listen to music or drive around the block one more time to get into that frame of mind—do it. Children are waiting for you to walk in the door and be with them. Bear hugs, eye contact, and focus are needed. They want to tell you about their day.

- **Maximize transitions.** Make it a priority to use morning driving time and afternoon pick-up time to connect. In the morning, talk about what you will do together when you get home. In the afternoon, be intentional about finding out what your child did while he was away from you.

- **Make lunch notes special.** Tucking in a riddle or photo is a wonderful way to stay connected. For infants and toddlers who spend time with another caregiver, send along a laminated photo of you together, as well as a favorite comfort toy or blanket.

- **Keep tabs on priorities.** An older dad said, "If I could do it again, I wouldn't have answered the phone during dinner." Put the cell phones out of sight, and focus on your children when you're together. Children respect your needs. They just don't want the phone to be a regular member of the family.

- **Separate work and family.** If you work at home, set aside one area as your office and don't work elsewhere in your home. Children will understand when you are in your office that this means you are working. The physical boundary helps them understand that work time is needed. If possible, don't let children play in your work space. If you need to take a call, do so in the office rather than in the same room with the breakfast conversation. Simple boundaries can make a big difference.

- **Keep bedtime routines consistent.** Protect this time to connect with love and patience. This cuddle time is when hearts open up and your children talk with you about their feelings and ideas. The connection and peacefulness of this practice will pay off for both of you. Think of this as your time to wind down, as well.

Talk with positively about your work. Everyone has rough days, and it is important not to bring that home. It is incredibly easy to fall into the habit of complaining to a spouse or friend about a boss, the workload, the drive home, or other frustrations. Children are listening. So, let them hear the fun and interesting experiences you have. If you had a great lunch, describe what you ate. Talk about what you saw on your bus ride home. Keep your communication filled with new things you observed or learned. Children like to know what you enjoyed about your day.

Young children don't need to know and should be protected from worry about their parents' job security. They don't need to know that the bills are late or that you are anxious. They can see from your restraint in buying things that you are being careful. It isn't the things that matter; your attitude of gratitude will leave the greatest impression.

You can keep your connections strong by sharing a positive spirit about your need to be away. Celebrate the moments when you come back together. There are no happier words than, "Daddy's home!" or "Mommy's home!" You can make your children feel special and loved, even when you are apart.

Learning to Slow Down

With us, it's always, "Hurry!" Just hearing that word stresses me out. We often have five minutes to a deadline. We have to get in the car. I was telling the girls constantly, "Hurry, hurry, hurry." That freaked them out. I was always in crisis mode. We had to get out of the drama and get efficient in what we were doing. I realized I just had to turn this around.

David Elkind, author of *The Hurried Child*, suggests that children are hurried through life with pressures that are too great to handle and that lead to a lasting crisis. They wake up too early, don't get enough sleep, are hurried off to school, and then are shuffled to a stacked agenda of activities. Parents may mean well, but the result is tired children and exhausted families who are aiming for admirable goals but missing the mark.

Children need the years of childhood with lots of free time to let their imaginations blossom, to discover their passions, and to learn and grow through trial and error. They need to stretch out on the ground, watch the clouds overhead, and enjoy the lovely feeling of suspended time when nothing is pressing on them. They need your protection from the pressures of adult life that threaten to invade their childhood space.

Many times, the most damaging intrusion into the time you have is the pressure you feel when heading out the door. Patience is required for things to go smoothly. Telling funny stories and talking about unusual or interesting things can slow a moment down while accomplishing needed tasks.

A father of two young boys said, "We don't have as much money as our relatives. They went to a mountain cabin and got snowmobiles for their vacation. We realize we can't do that. But we have the basic tools and know how to have fun. We try to make the most of our time and make memories that don't cost money." All of us are given the same twenty-four hours in each day and can decide how we will spend it.

Slow the clock and enjoy being together. Children won't remember the things you let go of to spend time with them. They won't care that you didn't wash the dishes right after dinner, only that you put a puzzle together with them. Here are some ideas to get started:

- **Take a walk.** Look for birds, animals, people, or kinds of dogs. Breathe deeply. Hold hands. Listen to the wind. Take your baby or toddler for a walk in the stroller or carrier, and talk about what you see and hear.

- **Lie on the grass and look at clouds.** Talk about what you discover.

- **Read a book and talk about the pictures.** Imagine with your child that you could take objects out of the book or could go inside the book to play. What would you do?

> Take time. Be filled with patience. Stay in the moment. Make this happen by focusing on the present need. Make a priority of your child's spirit.

- **Lie on the floor together with a blanket and pillow.** Listen to beautiful music and tickle your child's arm, letting your fingers dance to the beat or soothe with the melody.

- **Call someone you love who lives in another place.** Talk via video chat, such as FaceTime or Skype, if possible. Enjoy talking with Grandpa or another family member you love.

- **Go visiting, or invite someone over.** Make it a tea party, and let your child help you set out different tea flavors, with muffins and tiny sandwiches on plates. Share stories about your own childhood, and let children tell you what they want to be when they grow up. The idea is to slow down the day, focus, and make it special.

- **Take time to play, explore, and be a child again.** Enjoy the simple things. Run, jump, and introduce your child to the activities you love. Encourage imagination and creativity, protecting time for their make-believe world. Whether it is a game of tag or kickball, joining in benefits you and them. Jump rope or do the Hokey Pokey or the bunny hop. Join in your children's dramatic scenes and take on the role of the pirate or magician. You—and they—will be glad you did.

These daily moments will add up to be the weeks and months of your lives. Your children will remember the joy you shared, no matter the pressing needs. What they really need most is time with you. But this mindset of staying in the moment will not happen without conscious effort and a determined commitment to enjoy your children.

Focusing on the Positive

> I want to do a better job at handling frustration with our children. I hate it when I resort to yelling. Then I watch them get mad at each other, and I feel guilty.

Owning your influence over how things turn out can help, especially because so much of life often feels out of control. A dad of five said, "I want each one of my children to feel they are the best part of my life and the happiest time of my day. I think about that as I juggle the many demands." There are things you cannot change and over which you will never have control. But you can change your words and your responses to challenges. It is stunning how much influence you have over your children's reactions by the way you respond yourself. Following are three helpful tips to help you maximize your influence in the way things turn out.

- **Guard your words.** Don't say everything you think or feel. Honesty is good, but self-restraint makes for great parenting. Children don't need to hear that you are anxious about driving in the rain. They don't need to know that your checkbook balance is low. They are enjoying childhood and deserve a day without your worry. An Arabic proverb advises, "Open your mouth only if what you are going to say is more beautiful than silence." Aim to talk less and listen more. Your children are not your friends; they are in your care. Save personal adult feelings for adult friends or your significant other.

- **Postpone answers**. Generally, you don't need to give an answer right away. Children are filled with ideas and energy. It helps to say, "That's a good idea. Let me think about that for a while." This gives you time to weigh your options and make a decision that you can stick with.

- **Make a nonevent out of unimportant experiences.** A mom of seven- and eight-year-old boys shared, "When I was with my sons in the car, they were so grumpy. One complained about having to run errands with me. The other was grumbling about his brother's feet in his space. I felt upset, because I had left work early to take them to get school supplies. I realized I could either fuss at them or let it go. Instead, I said, 'Grandma is coming at six. What should we have for dinner?' The boys forgot about their scuffle and told me they were hungry for pizza." In the moments when things are going wrong, you can change the subject and make a nonevent out of an unimportant issue. You can turn things around by shifting the focus.

> React in a surprising way. Tell a joke. Do jumping jacks. It is amazing how, when your head is cleared, you can think better and decide on a more creative way to handle a situation.

You can turn around a situation almost immediately by having fun. You can change an ordinary moment into an extraordinary one by doing the unexpected. Infusing joy and humor into what might otherwise be a difficult situation or a boring afternoon will create memories that will leave an impression for years to come.

Looking Back and Seeing Forward

Some days, I feel that nothing is going the way I planned it. I know the boys are going to grow beyond these unpredictable times quickly. I want to enjoy them and stay in the moment. To deal with the challenges, I have to show up and stay present.

When all has been said and done and your children leave for college or careers, you will realize that parenting was probably the greatest adventure of your life. In trying to raise your children, you will have learned so much. When you look back on the roller coaster, the ups and downs, the trying times and the joys, you will know it was worth the ride.

Your little humans really are outstanding—their amazing belly laughter as babies, their sense of humor and delight as toddlers, their crazy energy and explosion of learning and fun in the preschool years. They came into life as their own persons, with unique perspectives, endless insights, and a one-of-a kind personalities. Build a foundation of love and help them become truly caring and generous. Don't sweat the small stuff, and focus more on things that matter.

Parenting may seem like a constant responsibility that will be here forever. But as your children grow, you will find you have developed a deeper understanding about parenting. In the fullest sense, you will have learned how to protect, guide, influence, teach, lead, and inspire. You will have progressed from being a novice to being a competent nurturer, mentor, and coach. The essential connection and secure attachment you have nurtured throughout childhood is the bedrock on which all other parts of the parenting journey rest. This bridge of connection gives children an enduring way home that allows them to venture forth on their pathway to maturity with confidence and to return to our safety and support when needed. They know that their connection to home and family is unchanging and that you will always be there for them.

When children's need for belonging and significance is rooted deeply in your family identity, they will feel secure in the teen years ahead. When they have experienced a positive relationship with you, they will understand how good it feels to be safe, protected, and loved. In the future, this is the kind of love that they will seek with others, and this is the kind of love that they will be able to give. This perspective can help you breathe deeply and keep your eyes on the horizon when you reach the top of the ride, in anticipation of the thrilling descent. As you grip the bar and hang on, don't forget the bigger picture—the path of life moving ever forward.

Aiming for the Future

We were so caught up in that day-to-day rush, and I seriously wondered if all of this effort was making a difference. Were my kids getting anything at all that I wanted them to learn? That day they went with my mother.

She called me later to tell me, "Aubrey is imitating everything you say. You may not see it, but she sure is. When we were making lunch, Aubrey said to me over and over, 'My mommy said do it like this . . . My mommy said put it like that.'" My mom reminded me that just because I don't see it right away doesn't mean it's not taking root.

Life with others can be complex, so our words of compassion for each other really matter. Make your home a life-giving place where there is consistent care and kindness. Teach your children that love multiplies and adds and does not divide or subtract. Know that, day after day, you are shaping the life of your child.

As you reflect and plan for the months and years ahead, know for sure that each moment offers you a chance for a fresh start. Be inspired to grow along with your children, setting new goals and moving ahead with purpose and vision. You can't determine the future, but you can make the best possible today for yourself and your children.

When your children look at your face when they struggle, let them see hope, love, and confidence, rather than fear or worry. They will borrow your confidence while they build confidence in themselves. Your words of approval and acceptance will fill them with the belief that they can do it.

When hard times come, you can change the direction of your children's lives by saying, "When you get through this, you will have so many new skills." "You are learning so much about being a good friend." "I am proud of the way you handled this situation."

When you realize that nurturing and empowering your children must start with you, it is an incredible moment of truth in your parenting journey. This is a level of selfless love and service that nothing else prepares you for. It is within your power to chart a course of blessing for your children. Fill your home with laughter and your children's hearts with patient love. You will go forward and leave a legacy of strength and security that will empower your children for life.

RECOMMENDED CHILDREN'S BOOKS

As you identify areas where you could support your child's developing strengths and resilience, the following books can help you have conversations with your children about changes, emotions, loss, and other topics. Some of the books are out of print, but most will be available at your local public library.

Adoption

Cole, Joanna. 1995. *How I Was Adopted*. New York: Morrow Junior Books.

Curtis, Jamie Lee. 1996. *Tell Me Again about the Night I Was Born*. New York: HarperCollins.

Katz, Karen. 1997. *Over the Moon: An Adoption Tale*. New York: Henry Holt.

Lewis, Rose. 2000. *I Love You Like Crazy Cakes*. Boston, MA: Little Brown.

Lin, Grace. 2007. *The Red Thread: An Adoption Fairy Tale*. Morton Grove, IL: Albert Whitman.

Richmond, Marianne. 2008. *I Wished for You: An Adoption Story*. Naperville, IL: Sourcebooks.

Rogers, Fred. 1998. *Let's Talk About It: Adoption*. New York: Putnam and Grosset.

Bereavement and Loss

Bunting, Eve. 2000. *The Memory String*. New York: Clarion.

Cobb, Rebecca. 2011. *Missing Mommy: A Book about Bereavement.* New York: Henry Holt.

Mundy, Michaelene. 2006. *Sad Isn't Bad: A Good-Grief Guidebook for Kids Dealing with Loss.* St. Meinrad, IN: Abbey Press.

Mundy, Michaelene. 2009. *What Happens When Someone Dies: A Child's Guide to Death and Funerals.* St. Meinrad, IN: Abbey Press.

Ryan, Victoria. 2002. *When Your Grandparent Dies: A Child's Guide to Good Grief.* St. Meinrad, IN: Abbey Press.

Shriver, Maria. 1999. *What's Heaven?* New York: St. Martin's Press.

Shriver, Maria. 2004. *What's Happening to Grandpa?* New York: Little Brown.

Calming Anger and Frustration

Agassi, Martine. 2002. *Hands Are Not for Hitting.* Minneapolis, MN: Free Spirit.

Bang, Molly. 1999. *When Sophie Gets Angry—Really, Really Angry.* New York: Blue Sky Press.

Berry, Joy. 2013. *Let's Talk about Feeling Angry.* Wheaton, IL: Watkins.

deRubertis, Barbara. 2011. *Tessa Tiger's Temper Tantrums.* New York: Kane Press.

Meiners, Cheri. 2005. *Talk and Work It Out.* Minneapolis, MN: Free Spirit.

Preston, Edna. 1976. *The Temper Tantrum Book.* New York: Puffin.

Spelman, Cornelia. 2000. *When I Feel Angry.* Morton Grove, IL: Albert Whitman.

Vail, Rachel. 2002. *Sometimes I'm Bombaloo.* New York: Scholastic.

Verdick, Elizabeth. 2010. *Calm-Down Time.* Minneapolis, MN: Free Spirit.

Character and Kindness

Asael, Anthony, and Stephanie Rabemiafara. 2011. *Children of the World: How We Live, Learn, and Play in Poems, Drawings, and Photographs.* New York: Universe.

Coe, Julie. 2009. *The Friendship Puzzle: Helping Kids Learn about Accepting and Including Kids with Autism.* Blue Bell, PA: Larstan.

Cooper, Ilene. 2002. *The Golden Rule.* New York: Abrams.

Curtis, Jamie Lee. 2006. *Is There Really a Human Race?* New York: HarperCollins.

Fox, Mem. 2006. *Whoever You Are.* Boston, MA: HMH Books for Young Readers.

Gainer, Cindy. 1998. *I'm Like You, You're Like Me: A Child's Book About Understanding and Celebrating Each Other.* Minneapolis, MN: Free Spirit.

Lewis, Beverly. 2007. *In Jesse's Shoes.* Bloomington, MN: Bethany House.

McCloud, Carol. 2015. *Have You Filled a Bucket Today? A Guide to Daily Happiness for Kids.* Brighton, MI: Bucket Fillers.

Pak, Soyung. 2003. *Sumi's First Day of School Ever.* New York: Viking.

Pearson, Emily. 2002. *Ordinary Mary's Extraordinary Deed.* Layton, UT: Gibbs Smith.

Thomas, Pat. 2002. *Don't Call Me Special: A First Look at Disability.* Hauppauge, NY: Barron's Educational.

Divorce

Girard, Linda. 1987. *At Daddy's on Saturdays.* Morton Grove, IL: Albert Whitman.

Krasny Brown, Laurene. 1986. *Dinosaurs Divorce: A Guide for Changing Families.* New York: Little Brown.

Lansky, Vicki. 1998. *It's Not Your Fault, Koko Bear.* Minnetonka, MN: Book Peddlers.

Levins, Sandra, and Bryan Langdo. 2005. *Was It the Chocolate Pudding? A Story for Little Kids about Divorce.* Washington, DC: Magination Press.

Masurel, Claire. 2001. *Two Homes.* Cambridge, MA: Candlewick Press.

Ransom, Jeanie. 2000. *I Don't Want to Talk about It.* Washington, DC: Magination Press.

Rogers, Fred. 1998. *Let's Talk About It: Divorce.* New York: Penguin Putnam for Young Readers.

Spelman, Cornelia. 1998. *Mama and Daddy Bear's Divorce.* Morton Grove, IL: Albert Whitman.

Expressing Emotions

Browning-Wroe, Jo. 2006. *Happy, Sad, Jealous, Mad: Stories, Rhymes, and Activities that Help Young Children Understand Their Emotions.* Minneapolis, MN: Key Education.

Cain, Janan. 2000. *The Way I Feel.* Seattle, WA: Parenting Press.

Curtis, Jamie Lee. 2007. *I'm Gonna Like Me: Letting Off a Little Self-Esteem.* New York: HarperCollins.

Curtis, Jamie Lee. 2007. *Today I Feel Silly and Other Moods That Make My Day.* New York: HarperCollins.

Fox, Mem. 2003. *Harriet, You'll Drive Me Wild!* Boston, MA: HMH Books for Young Readers.

Hoffman, Mary. 2013. *The Great Big Book of Feelings.* London, UK: Frances Lincoln Children's.

Rylant, Cynthia. 2002. *The Ticky-Tacky Doll.* Orlando, FL: Harcourt.

Viorst, Judith. 1987. *Alexander and the Terrible, Horrible, No Good, Very Bad Day.* New York: Aladdin.

Illness

Bostrom, Kathleen. 2004. *When Pete's Dad Got Sick: A Book about Chronic Illness.* Grand Rapids, MI: Zonderkidz.

Bourgeois, Paulette. 2000. *Franklin Goes to the Hospital.* Toronto: Kids Can Press.

Duncan, Debbie. 1994. *When Molly Was in the Hospital: A Book for Brothers and Sisters of Hospitalized Children.* Windsor, CA: Rayve Productions.

McKeever, Stacia. 2006. *Why Is Keiko Sick? A Conversation with Your Child about Why Bad Things Happen.* Green Forest, AR: Master Books.

Rivlin-Gutman, Annette. 2006. *Mommy Has to Stay in Bed.* North Charleston, SC: BookSurge.

New Sibling

Anholt, Laurence. 1995. *Sophie and the New Baby.* London, UK: Orchard.

Berenstain, Jan, and Stan Berenstain. 1974. *The Berenstain Bears' New Baby.* New York: Random House.

Danzig, Dianne. 2009. *Babies Don't Eat Pizza: A Big Kids' Book about Baby Brothers and Baby Sisters.* New York: Dutton Children's Books.

Mayer, Mercer. 1983. *The New Baby.* New York: Golden Books.

Munsch, Robert. 1986. *Love You Forever.* Buffalo, NY: Firefly.

Rosenberg, Maxine. 1997. *Mommy's in the Hospital Having a Baby.* New York: Clarion.

Sarah, Duchess of York. 2010. *Michael and His New Baby Brother.* New York: Sterling.

Schindel, John. 1998. *Frog Face: My Little Sister and Me.* New York: Henry Holt.

Scott, Ann Herbert. 1992. *On Mother's Lap.* New York: Clarion.

Woodson, Jacqueline. 2010. *Pecan Pie Baby.* New York: Putnam.

REFERENCES AND RECOMMENDED READINGS

American Academy of Pediatrics. 2016. "Media and Children." https://www.aap.org/en-us/advocacy-and-policy/aap-health-initiatives/Pages/Media-and-Children.aspx

Bowlby, Richard. 2008. "Attachment Theory: How to Help Young Children Acquire a Secure Attachment." In Michiel Matthes, *The Report of the Seventh Session of the Working Group on the Quality of Childhood within the European Parliament.* Brussels, Belgium: Alliance for Childhood European Network Group. Excerpt retrieved from http://www.allianceforchildhood.eu/files/QOC%20Sig%204.pdf

Bronson, Po, and Ashley Merryman. 2013. *Top Dog: The Science of Winning and Losing.* New York: Hachette.

Center on the Developing Child. 2015. *InBrief: The Impact of Early Adversity on Children's Development.* Cambridge, MA: Harvard University. Retrieved from www.developingchild.harvard.edu.

Centers for Disease Control. 2014. *Essentials for Childhood: Steps to Create Safe, Stable, Nurturing Relationships and Environments.* Washington, DC: National Center for Injury Prevention and Control, Division of Violence Prevention. Retrieved from http://www.cdc.gov/violenceprevention/pdf/essentials_for_childhood_framework.pdf

Child Maltreatment and Violence Committee. 2012. *Policy Statement on Corporal Punishment.* American Academy of Child and Adolescent Psychiatry. https://www.aacap.org/aacap/policy_statements/2012/Policy_Statement_on_Corporal_Punishment.aspx

Christakis, Dimitri, et al. 2014. "Early Television Exposure and Subsequent Attentional Problems in Children." *Pediatrics* 113(4): 708–713.

Coles, Robert. 1990. *The Spiritual Life of Children.* Boston: Houghton Mifflin.

Cozolino, Louis. 2006. *The Neuroscience of Human Relationships: Attachment and the Developing Social Brain.* New York: W. W. Norton.

Duckworth, Angela, Eli Tsukayama, and Teri Kirby. 2013. "Is It Really Self-Control? Examining the Predictive Power of the Delay of Gratification Task." *Personality and Social Psychology Bulletin* 39(7): 843–855.

Dweck, Carol. 2007. "The Perils and Promises of Praise." *Early Intervention at Every Age* 65(2): 34–39. http://www.ascd.org/publications/educational-leadership/oct07/vol65/num02/The-Perils-and-Promises-of-Praise.aspx

Elkind, David. 2001. *The Hurried Child: Growing Up Too Fast Too Soon*. 3rd ed. Boston: Da Capo Press.

Evans, Angela, and Kang Lee. 2013. "Emergence of Lying in Very Young Children." *Developmental Psychology* 49(10): 1958–1963.

Fink, Jennifer. 2011. "I Didn't Do It!" *Scholastic Parent and Child* 19(3): 59–62.

Gershoff, Elizabeth. 2010. "More Harm than Good: A Summary of Scientific Research on the Intended and Unintended Effects of Corporal Punishment on Children." *Law and Contemporary Problems* 73(31): 31–56.

Gershoff, Elizabeth, and Andrew Grogan-Kaylor. 2016. "Spanking and Child Outcomes: Old Controversies and New Meta-Analyses." *Journal of Family Psychology*. Advance online publication. http://dx.doi.org/10.1037/fam0000191

Gopnik, Alison, Andrew Meltzoff, and Patricia Kuhl. 1999. *The Scientist in the Crib: What Early Learning Tells Us about the Mind*. New York: William Morrow.

Green, James, Pamela Whitney, and Michael Potegal. 2011. "Screaming, Yelling, Whining, and Crying: Categorical and Intensity Differences in Vocal Expressions of Anger and Sadness in Children's Tantrums." *Emotion* 11(5): 1124–1133.

Haiman, Peter. 1998. "The Case Against Time-Out." *Mothering* 88(3): 34.

Haugen, Kirsten. 2015. "The Unteachable Moment: Lessons from the Neuroscience of Stress, Conflict, and (Mis)behavior." *Beginnings Professional Development Workshop*. Child Care Exchange. https://ccie-catalog.s3.amazonaws.com/library/5022148.pdf

Heitin, Liana. 2013. "U.S. Achievement Stalls as Other Nations Make Gains." *Education Week* December 3. Retrieved from http://www.edweek.org/ew/articles/2013/12/03/14pisa.h33.html

Hirshkowitz, Max, et al. 2015. "National Sleep Foundation's Sleep Time Duration Recommendations: Methodology and Results Summary." *Sleep Health* 1(1): 40–43.

Howard, Eboni. 2015. *What Matters Most for Children: Influencing Inequality at the Start of Life*. Research report. Washington DC: American Institutes for Research. Retrieved from http://www.air.org/sites/default/files/downloads/report/Early-Childhood-Education-Equity-Howard-August-2015.pdf

Institute of Medicine. 2011. *Early Childhood Obesity Prevention Policies: Goals, Recommendations and Potential Actions*. Washington, DC: National Academies of Science, Engineering, and Medicine.

Joussemet, Mireille, Renee Landry, and Richard Koestner. 2008. "A Self-Determination Theory Perspective on Parenting." *Canadian Psychology* 49(3): 194–200.

Kelly, Yvonne, John Kelly, and Amanda Sacker. 2013. "Changes in Bedtime Schedules and Behavioral Difficulties in Seven-Year-Old Children." *Pediatrics* 132(5): 1184–1193.

Kersey, Katharine, and Marie Masterson. 2010. "Is Tattling a Bad Word? How to Help Children Navigate the Playground." *Childhood Education* 86(4): 260–263.

Kochanska, Grazyna, et al. 2013. "Promoting Toddlers' Positive Social-Emotional Outcomes in Low-Income Families: A Play-Based Experimental Study." *Journal of Clinical Child and Adolescent Psychology* 42(4): 700–712.

Kohn, Alfie. 1993. *Punished by Rewards: The Trouble with Gold Stars, Incentives Plans, A's, Praise, and Other Bribes*. Boston: Houghton Mifflin.

Landry, Susan, Karen Smith, and Paul Swank. 2006. "Responsive Parenting: Establishing Early Foundations for Social, Communication, and Independent Problem-Solving Skills." *Developmental Psychology* 42(4): 627–642.

Landry, Susan, et al. 2008. "A Responsive Parenting Intervention: The Optimal Timing across Early Childhood for Impacting Maternal Behaviors and Child Outcomes." *Developmental Psychology* 44(5): 1335–1353.

Leong, Deborah, and Elena Bodrova. 2012. "Assessing and Scaffolding Make-Believe Play." *Young Children* 67(1): 28–34.

Lerner, Claire, and Lynette Ciervo. 2010. "Parenting Young Children Today: What the Research Tells Us." *Zero to Three* 30(4): 4–9.

Lillard, Angeline, and Jennifer Peterson. 2011. "The Immediate Impact of Different Types of Television on Young Children's Executive Function." *Pediatrics* 128(4): 644–649.

Lu, Stephanie. 2015. "From Lying Children to Successful Adults." *The Wilson Quarterly.* Retrieved from http://wilsonquarterly.com/stories/from-lying-children-to-successful-adults/

Manganello, Jennifer, and Catherine Taylor. 2009. "Television Exposure as a Risk Factor for Aggressive Behavior among Three-Year-Old Children." *Archives of Pediatric and Adolescent Medicine* 163(11): 1037–1045.

Miller, Alice. 2001. *The Truth Will Set You Free: Overcoming Emotional Blindness and Finding Your True Adult Self.* New York: Basic Books.

Mills, Rosemary, et al. 2008. "Cortisol Reactivity and Regulation Associated with Shame Responding in Early Childhood." *Developmental Psychology* 44(8): 1369–1380.

Mindell, Jodi, et al. 2009. "A Nightly Bedtime Routine: Impact on Sleep in Young Children and Maternal Mood." *Journal of Sleep and Sleep Disorders Research* 32(5): 599–606.

Mischel, Walter. 2014. *The Marshmallow Test: Why Self-Control Is the Engine of Success.* New York: Little, Brown.

Moreno, Sylvain, et al. 2011. "Short-Term Music Training Enhances Verbal Intelligence and Executive Function." *Psychological Science* 22(11): 1425–1433.

Narvaez, Darcia. 2010. "The Emotional Foundations of High Moral Intelligence." In Brigitte Latzko and Tina Malti, eds., *Children's Moral Emotions and Moral Cognition: Developmental and Educational Perspectives,* vol. 129. San Francisco: Jossey-Bass.

National Center for Children in Poverty. 2016. *Child Poverty.* New York: Columbia University. Retrieved from http://www.nccp.org/topics/childpoverty.html

National Scientific Council on the Developing Child. 2005/2014. *Excessive Stress Disrupts the Architecture of the Developing Brain: Working Paper No. 3.* Updated edition. Cambridge, MA: Harvard University. www.developingchild.harvard.edu

National Scientific Council on the Developing Child. 2011. *Building the Brain's "Air Traffic Control" System: How Early Experiences Shape the Development of Executive Function: Working Paper No. 11.* Cambridge, MA: Harvard University. www.developingchild.harvard.edu

Newsweek staff. 2004. "Clean Freaks." *Newsweek,* June 4. http://www.newsweek.com/clean-freaks-129009

Parlakian, Rebecca, and Claire Lerner. 2010. "Beyond 'Twinkle, Twinkle': Using Music with Infants and Toddlers." *Young Children* 65(2): 14–19.

Pate, Russell, et al. 2013. "Top 10 Research Questions Related to Physical Activity in Preschool Children." *Research Quarterly for Exercise and Sport* 84(4): 448–455.

Pew Research Center. 2014. *Teaching the Children: Sharp Ideological Differences, Some Common Ground.* Washington, DC: Pew Research Center. Available at http://www.people-press.org/files/2014/09/09-18-14-Child-Rearing-Values-Release.pdf

Philbrook, Lauren, et al. 2014. "Maternal Emotional Availability at Bedtime and Infant Cortisol at 1 and 3 Months." *Early Human Development* 90(10): 595–603.

Pink, Daniel. 2005. *A Whole New Mind: Why Right-Brainers Will Rule the Future.* New York: Penguin.

Raby, Lee, et al. 2014. "The Enduring Predictive Significance of Early Maternal Sensitivity: Social and Academic Competence through Age Thirty-Two Years." *Child Development* 86(3): 695–708.

Ray, Sharon. 2006. "Mother-Toddler Interactions during Child-Focused Activity in Transitional Housing." *Occupational Therapy in Health Care* 20(3–4): 81–97.

Stipek, Deborah, and Kathy Seal. 2001. *Motivated Minds: Raising Children Who Love Learning.* New York: Henry Holt.

Story, Mary, and Simone French. 2004. "Food Advertising and Marketing Directed at Children and Adolescents in the US." *International Journal of Behavior, Nutrition, and Physical Activity* 1(3): 1–17.

Suskind, Dana. 2015. *Thirty Million Words: Building a Child's Brain.* New York: Dutton.

Suskind, Dana et al. 2013. *Bridging the Early Language Gap: A Plan for Scaling Up.* White paper. Chicago, IL: University of Chicago. Retrieved from http://harris.uchicago.edu/sites/default/files/White%20Paper%20Suskind_Leffel_Landry_Cunha%209%2030%2020131.pdf

Szente, Judit. 2007. "Empowering Young Children for Success in School and in Life." *Early Childhood Education Journal* 34(6): 449–453.

Talwar, Victoria, and Kang Lee. 2008. "Social and Cognitive Correlates of Children's Lying Behavior." *Child Development* 79(4): 866–881.

Talwar, Victoria, Cindy Arruda, and Sarah Yachison. 2015. "The Effects of Punishment and Appeals for Honesty on Children's Truth-Telling Behavior." *Journal of Experimental Child Psychology* 130(1): 209–217.

Twenge, Jean, and Keith Campbell. 2008. "Increases in Positive Self-Views among High School Students: Birth-Cohort Changes in Anticipated Performance, Self-Satisfaction, Self-Liking, and Self-Competence. *Psychological Science* 19(11): 1082–1086.

UNICEF. 2014. *Building Better Brains: New Frontiers in Early Childhood Development.* New York: United Nations Children Fund. Retrieved from http://www.unicef.org/earlychildhood/files/Building_better_brains_web.pdf

University of Michigan Health System. 2016. "Television and Children." *YourChild Development and Behavior Resources: A Guide to Information and Support for Parents.* Retrieved from http://www.med.umich.edu/yourchild/topics/tv.htm

Waite, Sue, and Sarah Rees. 2014. "Practising Empathy: Enacting Alternative Perspectives through Imaginative Play." *Cambridge Journal of Education* 44(1): 1–18.

Wilking, Cara. 2011. *Issue Brief: Reining in Pester Power Food and Beverage Marketing.* Boston, MA: The Public Health Advocacy Institute, Northeastern University School of Law. Retrieved from http://www.phaionline.org/wp-content/uploads/2011/09/Pester_power.pdf

Zero to Three. 2009. *Parenting Infants and Toddlers Today: Research Findings Based on a Survey among Parents of Children Ages Birth to Three Years Old.* Washington, DC: Hart Research Associates.

Zimmerman, Frederick, Dimitri Christakis, and Andrew Meltzoff. 2007. "Associations between Media Viewing and Language Development in Children under Age Two Years." *Journal of Pediatrics* 151(4): 364–368.

Zimmerman, Frederick, et al. 2005. "Early Cognitive Stimulation, Emotional Support, and Television Watching as Predictors of Subsequent Bullying among Grade-School Children." *Archives of Pediatric and Adolescent Medicine* 159(4): 384–388.

INDEX

G

Generosity, 167–168
Gifts and talents, 102–105
Good habits, 18, 21
Gratitude, 18, 64, 124, 165–167
Grief and loss, 124–126, 191–192
Guidance, 69–70, 73

H

Handling failure, 116–117
Health, 15–16, 33, 64, 70–71, 121, 145–147
Helping others, 60, 78, 85–105, 115, 167–168
Hitting, 142–144
Holidays, 172
Homework, 40, 57
Honesty, 112–113, 161–165, 186–187
Honoring childhood, 84, 184–186
Humor, 18, 33, 39–40, 61, 70, 86, 104, 108, 131–132,
    173–181, 187

I

"I love you" notes, 181, 183
"I" messages, 177
Identifying emotions, 26–27, 29, 81, 91, 93–96, 110–113,
    132, 134–136, 142–144, 153–154, 164, 177, 193–194
Illness, 26, 71, 122–124, 133, 148, 194
Immediate gratification, 62–64
Impulsive behavior, 64–65, 96, 159–161
Incentives, 78
Inconsistency, 50, 73, 133, 148
Independence, 53, 76, 99–100, 141
Internalizing, 9–10, 108

J

Jealousy, 114, 119–122, 140–142
Job loss, 118–119
Journaling, 8, 42, 92–93, 166
Judgment, 26

K

Kindness, 10, 13, 18, 50, 65, 70, 114, 116, 154, 156–157,
    192–193

L

Labels, 19
Language development, 28–31, 42, 52–53, 59, 62, 86,
    90–96, 132, 140, 143, 155, 157, 166
Laughter, 7, 61, 86
Listening, 29–30, 32, 141, 186–187

M

Make-believe, 53
Making assumptions, 176

Making excuses, 140–142
Making memories, 21–22, 29–30, 31, 40–43, 61–62,
    171–174
Making mistakes, 65, 70–71, 154
Managing risks, 108–110, 157–159
Manners, 56, 61–62, 84
Massage, 34, 37
Meal times, 31–32, 34–35, 39, 41, 46–47, 51, 62, 78,
    146–147, 172, 180, 183
Meltdowns, 26, 38–41, 109, 132–134, 148–149
Memory books, 180
Mental health and physical punishment, 68–69
Messes, 14, 103–105
Military deployments, 118–119
Mirroring, 22
Modeling behaviors, 12–13, 15, 18, 29, 42, 49–50, 70–71,
    76, 86, 95, 115, 136, 143, 147, 153–155, 160, 163–
    165, 175–177
Mornings, 16–17, 77
Motivating effort, 98–100

N

Name calling, 80
Narrating what works, 101, 155, 157
Nighttime waking, 37, 144–145
Nonverbal cues, 160–161
Noticing success, 48–49, 58, 80–82, 89, 92, 95, 101–102,
    120, 136, 148–149, 156–157
Nutrition, 15–16, 64, 70–71, 146–147

O

One-on-one time, 33, 59–60, 121–122, 124, 142
Organization, 57–58, 89, 97
Out-of-control behavior, 135–136
Oxytocin, 30–32

P

Pacifiers, 36, 143
Pain, 68–69
Parental influence, 1, 4–5, 9–10, 12–13, 25–43, 70–71,
    109–110, 127–129
Parentese, 29
Patience, 13–15, 17–18, 30, 32, 52, 65, 70, 87, 108, 128,
    159–161, 174–175, 185
Peer pressure, 20–23, 57–58, 113–116
Perfectionism, 17–19, 178–179
Persistence, 98–100, 103
Personal style, 5–7, 14, 20–23, 25–27, 35, 51, 144–147,
    169
              character qualities, 18–19, 151–170
Personal-care issues, 144–147
Personality/temperament, 103–105, 181–182, 188
Pestering, 62–64, 131, 134
Pets, 33, 124–126
"Pinterest stress," 57
Planning ahead, 45–47, 55–56, 89, 99–100

T

Taking notes, 6, 8, 21, 42, 148
Talking softly, 56, 132
Teasing, 8, 113–116, 154, 156–157
Technology, 15, 60–62, 95, 159–160
Teething rings, 143
Thank-you notes, 166
Threats, 72–73
Time-out vs. taking a break, 136
Tiredness, 54–55, 133–134, 149, 176
Toilet training, 121, 145–146
Touch, 31–32, 34, 94
Traditions, 21–23, 31, 40–41, 166, 171–174
Transitions, 26, 29, 34, 38–41, 77, 112, 119–122, 127–129, 142–144, 148, 183

Trauma, 110–111
Trust, 36, 41–43, 59, 82, 116, 129

V

Victim role, 15

W

Waiting, 55, 63, 65, 98, 159–161
Warmth, 39
Whispering, 56, 64

Y

Yelling, 67–68, 70, 109, 132, 186